INTERIOR DESIGNERS AT HOME

STEPHEN CRAFTI

*Inspiration, Aesthetic, and Function
with 20 Top Global Designers*

Other Schiffer Books by the Author:
Second Home: A Different Way of Living, 978-0-7643-6596-6

Other Schiffer Books on Related Subjects:
The Forever Home: Designing Houses to Last a Lifetime, Boyce Thompson, 978-0-7643-6525-6

Copyright © 2024 by Stephen Crafti

Library of Congress Control Number: 2023941114

All rights reserved. No part of this work may be reproduced or used in any form or by any means—graphic, electronic, or mechanical, including photocopying or information storage and retrieval systems—without written permission from the publisher.

The scanning, uploading, and distribution of this book or any part thereof via the Internet or any other means without the permission of the publisher is illegal and punishable by law. Please purchase only authorized editions and do not participate in or encourage the electronic piracy of copyrighted materials.

"Schiffer," "Schiffer Publishing, Ltd.," and the pen and inkwell logo are registered trademarks of Schiffer Publishing, Ltd.

Edited by Jesse J. Marth
Designed by Molly Shields

On the Front Cover: From Thomas Geerling's home, *photo by Kasia Gtakowska*
On the Back Cover: *Top*: From Tim Van Steenbergen's home, *photo by Tijs Vervecken for Nome Furniture*; *Bottom left*: From Thomas Geerling's home, *photo by Kasia Gtakowska*; and *Bottom right*: From Gabriela Gargano's home, *photo by Kristen Francis*
Other Images: Title Page: From Allison Pye's home, *photo by Jack Shelton*; *p. 4*: From John Marx and Nikki Beach's home, *photo by Toni Garbasso*; *p. 7*: From Tatjana Sprick's home, *photo by Line Klein Studio*; *p. 8*: From Wesley Moon's home, *photo by Pernille Loof*; *p. 11*: From Tim Van Steenbergen's home, *photos by Tijs Vervecken for Nome Furniture*; *p. 12*: From Allison Pye's home, *photo by Jack Shelton*; *p. 84*: From Kate Challis's home, *photo of Valerie Sparks's* Le Vol *by Sharyn Cairns*; and *p. 166*: From Wesley Moon's home, *photo by Pernille Loof*

Type set in Bilo/Miller Text

ISBN: 978-0-7643-6738-0
Printed in China

Published by Schiffer Publishing, Ltd.
4880 Lower Valley Road
Atglen, PA 19310
Phone: (610) 593-1777; Fax: (610) 593-2002
Email: info@schifferbooks.com
Web: www.schifferbooks.com

For our complete selection of fine books on this and related subjects, please visit our website at www.schifferbooks.com. You may also write for a free catalog.

Schiffer Publishing's titles are available at special discounts for bulk purchases for sales promotions or premiums. Special editions, including personalized covers, corporate imprints, and excerpts, can be created in large quantities for special needs. For more information, contact the publisher.

I would like to dedicate this book to my partner, Naomi, who has been on this design journey with me over decades. Her support has been invaluable.

CONTENTS

6   Acknowledgments

8   Introduction

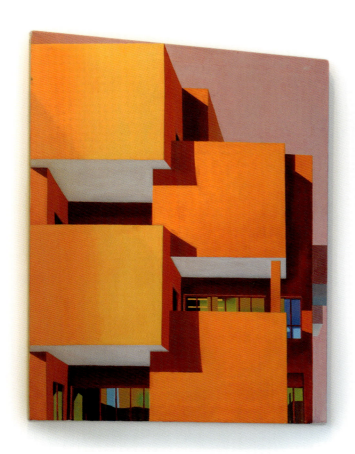

12 **INSPIRATION**

14 **TATJANA SPRICK**
A Curatorial Approach
Germany

26 **ALLISON PYE**
Layered with Memories of Travel
Australia

38 **TINA ENGELEN**
Beyond Fashion
Australia

48 **JOHN MARX AND NIKKI BEACH**
Looking Out through Mondrian's Window
United States of America

60 **ANDREW SHEINMAN**
Respecting the Past
United States of America

72 **ANDREW PARR**
A European Sensibility with a Contemporary Touch
Australia

84 AESTHETIC

86 KATE CHALLIS
Imbued with Color
Australia

98 SALLY MACKERETH
A Combo of John Lautner and Dickensian London
United Kingdom

110 TIM VAN STEENBERGEN
A Gem in Antwerp
Belgium

122 MICHAEL DEL PIERO
Minimalism inside a Beaux Arts Package
United States of America

134 EMILY GILLIS
Playing with Tones and Textures
Australia

144 CAROLE WHITING
Minimal but Textured
Australia

156 VICENTE WOLF
White-Hot Hell's Kitchen Loft
United States of America

166 FUNCTION

168 DOROTHY MEASER
Urban Pastoral House
United States of America

182 B.E ARCHITECTURE
Treated Like a House Rather Than an Apartment
Australia

194 THOMAS GEERLINGS
Canal House
The Netherlands

206 MELISSA DE CAMPO
A Ski Retreat
Australia

214 CANDACE BARNES
Views from the Top
United States of America

224 GABRIELA GARGANO
A Magical Oasis Developed over Time
United States of America

238 WESLEY MOON
Adding a Sense of Warmth
United States of America

254 Designer Directory

ACKNOWLEDGMENTS

I would like to thank all the designers and photographers featured in this book—without their talent, this book could not have been produced. I am also extremely appreciative of the photographers who so beautifully captured these homes, allowing each layer to be presented with their discerning eyes. I would also like to thank Joe Boschetti, who has assisted me during this process, together with Jesse Marth. Like Schiffer Publishing, they were a joy to work with.

My very special thanks to Fran Madigan for casting her eyes across the pages of this book. Your work is so greatly appreciated, Fran.

I hope this book will inspire you to look more closely at the world of interiors!

Stephen Crafti
Hon RAIA

ACKNOWLEDGMENTS 7

INTRODUCTION

I always imagined a career as an interior designer, putting together rooms for clients and showing which direction to go in. This never occurred, and I enrolled in town planning at college in the late 1970s: perhaps the closest thing to architecture and interior design; well, at least in my mind. But after working as a town planner in a local council for a couple of years, I knew that I had taken the wrong path—oh dear!

While it was a valuable learning experience, it wasn't design focused—with most of the time spent telling the public what was and what was not permissible in the urban environment. Fortunately, my partner was an excellent knitter, and so, in the early 1980s, I switched to becoming a knitwear designer—a terrific and creative experience that lasted until the end of that decade.

It was in the early 1990s when I purchased a modernist 1950s architect-designed house by Montgomery King & Trengove. This wonderful and inspiring home provided a new lease on life, while opening my third career as a writer, something that's continued to give me enormous pleasure ever since! Both seeing and writing about great architecture is simply a joy. How exciting it is to walk into someone's home and see how they live, whether it's a single person, a couple, or a family, traditional or hybrid.

This book takes the next step into the homes of some of the world's leading designers—showing us not only how they live and create magical spaces, but also some of the tricks of the trade—things to avoid as much as what to look out for. Some furniture and objects, for example, were purchased by these designers while traveling overseas, with even the smallest items being a touchstone for these travels, years later. Other designers have family heirlooms that have been passed down through the generations. And others simply have an eye and are quick enough to spot something special in a garage sale or even as scrap by the side of the road. There are also those designers who have family connections to top-end furniture showrooms that can create a seamless connection to the architecture.

I was eager to write this book for several reasons—while there are many fine books on interior design, most seem to focus on a certain look or style. There's the English / cottage style or French or perhaps Italian—showing how to follow and create your own home in this genre. However, I feel that interior design today, like fashion, which is now so wide and varied with so many ways of dressing, is such a melange of different looks and styles. Unlike, say, the 1960s, when the "space look" emerged, or in the 1970s, when caftans were the norm with Andre Courreges, fashion today is anything but predicable (but there is currently a dose of the 1970s).

When one turns the pages of this book, nothing is predictable. Take for instance, the home of interior designer Kate Challis, a converted shop that literally meets the pavement of an inner-city shopping strip. From gritty to fantastical (if such a word exists), her kitchen walls are literally embroidered with birds, not dissimilar to an aviary. Other homes, such as Tim Van Steenbergen's art nouveau home in Antwerp, are as breathtaking, with the front doors opening to a grand staircase illuminated by a glass ceiling. Each room of the period home has been meticulously restored. And the furniture, objects, and artifacts are as delightful, a combination of vintage finds and abstract paintings primarily from the 1950s and '60s. Interior designer Andrew Parr, director of SJB, also takes a spontaneous and personal approach in his own home, built a few years before Van Steenbergen's. Here, you'll find everything from original Pierre Cardin lamps from the 1970s that speak to Pierre Paulin's Groovy Chairs from the same period. And while many things are precious in Parr's home, he's certainly not concerned that the overscaled paper lamps in the informal lounge and above the indoor swimming pool are more for fun rather than being collectibles.

Some designers feature lavish interiors, while others, such as interior designer Carole Whiting, are pared back and minimal. There's a quietness both in Whiting's studio and her home above, with a neutral palette of colors and finishes—even the vitrine in her living area is tone on tone when it comes to the objects displayed. But in the quietness, there's certainly a richness of thought and a signature that can be found in many of her interiors.

Interior design isn't simply about having a good eye and knowing where to find things. It's about problem-solving. Thomas Geerlings's home on a canal in Amsterdam is testimony to the skills one requires as an interior designer. While there are five levels in his home, one that he shares with his wife and their children, each level is extremely small, with a footprint of only 538 square feet (50 square meters). Geerlings, as shown in this book, has managed to create a wonderful family home that feels considerably more spacious than it is. And while it doesn't have a lift or even a back garden, he manages to create a sense of the outdoors by including a glass ceiling in the kitchen, allowing the sky rather than vegetation to create a sense of the outdoors.

Other homes take the form of an apartment, something that's becoming more common as the price of detached houses (and many apartments) heads north. Interior designer Emily Gillis, for example, has created a magical interior in a pint-sized apartment, one that's only 538 square feet (50 square meters) in area. She removed the former window awnings and created a

palette of white on white by using subtle hues of white and various textures to add depth and interest. Others, such as designer Tina Engelen, who lives in the Grid in Sydney, exemplify the importance of doing things right from the outset rather than simply changing over new furniture every few years. Most of her furniture was purchased over twenty years ago, when the Grid was completed. The comfortable tan leather sofas and chairs look as fresh now as they did then.

When I look at the work produced by the designers included in this book, I am certainly aware of my shortcomings as an interior designer. Yes, I can write about what I see and experience. But that's a different set of skills from being a designer. This book will, I hope, give you some ideas that can be applied in your own home. As leading designers, they can afford to be considerably braver creating their own homes. These designers are guided by their experiences and aesthetics rather than strictly following a client's brief. And with this opportunity, certain rules can be ditched in favor of experimenting either with materials or spaces, or both. But be open to their ideas and take the journey with them, appreciating the way they stitch things together like no others, creating their own distinctive signatures in the process. Enjoy!

Stephen Crafti

INSPIRATION

TATJANA SPRICK
A CURATORIAL APPROACH

Schöneberg, Germany

Designer Tatjana Sprick's spacious apartment is in Schöneberg, a neighborhood in Berlin known for its many period buildings. Unlike some, where there have been inappropriate renovations, including shared lobbies, here virtually everything is beautifully intact—from the stained-glass windows to the ornate wood fretwork that greets one upon arrival. This experience continues up the staircase and can be found upon entering the apartment, filled with light that accentuates the home's decorative ceilings, sumptuous furniture, and objects. "I was looking for an apartment with generous light, as I mainly work from home when I'm in Berlin," says Tatjana, who regularly travels across Europe for work. "But I was also keen to live in an apartment that was larger than most you find here, to catch up with and entertain friends," she adds.

Tatjana previously worked in the fashion industry, working with Yohji Yamamoto; hence she lived in Paris for a considerable amount of time. So, while she wasn't expecting to re-create Paris in Schöneberg, Tatjana wanted to be close to shops and cafés, along with a park. "Schöneberg is quite central. It's easy for me to reach all parts of the city in a relatively short time, but it's also convenient to the trains which connect to the airport—which provides the ease of traveling through Europe," says Tatjana.

After traveling, what could be more relaxing than returning to this apartment with high decorative ceilings, pristine white walls in the formal areas, and wood parquetry floors. However, when Tatjana purchased this apartment, there were several changes that were made. It had been renovated in the mid-1970s by someone who considered themselves a handyperson (DIY approach). And while the aesthetic didn't correlate to the

The dining area also doubles as a meeting area for clients.

@tatjanasprick
Photos by Line Klein Studio

Opposite: Period and contemporary furniture complement each other.

Above left: The citrus-yellow velvet lounge found a new home in Sprick's apartment—a color that was difficult in finding a buyer.

Above right: In the living area, magazines are stacked up on a vintage tea trolley.

early-twentieth-century apartment, neither did the more pragmatic side, such as the outdated heating and electricity. Even the flooring, old carpet, was at odds with the original features. "I had already decorated a few flats before I purchased this one, so I had a fairly clear idea of what needed to be done," says Tatjana, who worked closely with BCO Architects.

The long and linear apartment features the living and dining areas at the front (the dining area doubles as a client meeting space), with the kitchen located at the core. The main bedroom and en suite is located at the rear. Although the rooms appear particularly large and the spaces fluid in their arrangement, several walls, particularly in the rear section of the apartment, were removed. The kitchen, which was initially located at the rear, was repositioned to the middle. This also allows greater separation between the private and more public areas in the apartment. The former kitchen then became the main bedroom. It is adjacent to a courtyard and is also a little quieter than if she had accommodated one of the front rooms, overlooking the street, as a bedroom.

Left: The living and dining rooms are located at the front of the apartment and are connected by period doors that were discovered during the renovation.

Right: The front entrance features a door with stained-glass lights and parquetry floors.

Opposite: Original doors were reinstated in the apartment.

Unlike some period-style apartments, where original features have been stripped out, here many were still intact. The old grimy carpet, for example, was removed and beautiful parquetry floors were discovered and simply sanded and oiled. Tatjana also removed all the rudimentary wooden shelves. "I couldn't believe that some of these exquisite ceilings were also concealed with false wood ceilings," says Tatjana, pointing out the intricate plasterwork. And while there were glass doors separating the dining area from the living areas that allowed light to pass through, Tatjana discovered an art nouveau door that is buried in a wall cavity from the turn of the twentieth century and is integral to the original architecture. "What was important for me was to enhance the light, particularly in the front rooms. And I was keen to create, by contrast, a more intimate kitchen," says Tatjana, who painted the kitchen in a dark emerald green and filled it with a delightful collection of objects and artifacts collected over many years and purchased in the many different countries she has traveled to. And rather than treat the kitchen as simply a utilitarian space, with its dramatic pendant light and objects on display, it has the feeling of an intimate dining space. It's also a contrast to the front rooms, which feature pristine white walls.

Having worked with a fashion designer who predominantly worked in black allowed Tatjana to move into color for her interiors. "Color is paramount. It also helps me delineate areas, whether it's for work or private areas for myself," says Tatjana. "I enjoy entertaining family and friends in rooms that feature warm and often-darker hues. And of course, I love ceramics and glass objects, which change with the light and help create a different mood."

Art and design also come to the fore in Tatjana's apartment, with a mélange of fascinating paintings, objects, and furniture. Local artists such as Julian Hoffmann are represented, along with a yellow chair by Eyal Burstein that was included in Design Miami in 2010. Then there's the distinctive yellow velvet sofa bought from Villa Harteneck, which, according to Tatjana, "nobody dared to buy." Other items are of less value but rekindle memories of places visited. Some furniture and objects were purchased at flea markets, both in Berlin and in other European cities, including a sideboard discovered in a vintage store in Berlin. Photography is also well represented in the apartment, including the work of Robert van der Hilst depicting a Chinese kitchen scene. "I just fell in love with it. It reminded me of Vermeer's colors," says Tatjana. Some things, such as a sofa that once belonged to her grandmother, was simply recovered from damaged blue silk to blue velvet. Other pieces, such as the Safari Chairs (circa 1950s), were also discovered in a local secondhand store. But many items come from far and wide, including Barcelona, Milan, and, in terms of the covers on the sofa, Istanbul. Tatjana also points out a photograph on the wall, taken by Monica Carocci, marking her last day at work at Yohji Yamamoto.

The office, adjacent to the dining room, also functions as a guest bedroom.

Opposite: A vintage bureau is paired with a midcentury office chair.

While each object or piece of furniture in Tatjana's apartment comes with a story or a place where it was purchased, for her the most challenging thing about this renovation was not damaging the original structure, whether it was the walls or revealing the exquisite floors below the old carpet. "I wanted to restore the apartment to its former glory, bringing back its original beauty. And it's now truly that!"

TIPS

What a home is or should be is very personal. Often, people get inspired by certain trends or looks that don't respond to the way a person or a family live.

Many are hesitant to use strong colors, whether on their walls or when selecting furniture. But as with my green kitchen walls or yellow sofa, they create a unique space. Some say, "Oh wow . . . that looks so amazing, but I would never have dared to buy it!"

Dark-green walls in the kitchen provide a perfect backdrop for Sprick's many objects and artifacts, including an extensive collection of vintage crockery and glassware.

Opposite: The kitchen sink is treated as a piece of furniture.

The main bedroom is located at the rear of the apartment.

Both the main bedroom and the adjacent bathroom are beautifully "layered."

ALLISON PYE
LAYERED WITH MEMORIES OF TRAVEL

Melbourne, Australia

As soon as you enter interior designer Allison's Pye home in the bayside Melbourne suburb of St. Kilda, you are immediately struck of someone well traveled. Objects and artifacts discovered while traveling abroad resonate as much as the things found locally. Each item comes with a story, and together they create a wonderful, layered home.

However, when Allison purchased this single-fronted house sixteen years ago, what was a Victorian-style dwelling was virtually unrecognizable. It had been renovated by the former owners in the 1960s, and apart from the two front rooms, everything had been changed. "It was literally a warren of rooms, very small ones at that. But it was the location, near the beach, that attracted me and of course this street, with its heritage-listed homes," says Allison, who lives here with her French bulldog, Peter Parker. As well as rooms being "dinky" (Allison's word), the color scheme throughout was mission brown: "Awful is all I can say," she adds.

It was referred to as the last renovated house on the street, and Allison worked with architect Susi Leeton in her mission to transform the place into a light-filled home and studio. The duo retained the two front rooms, separated by a fireplace, and virtually demolished the rest. This provided an opportunity to add a first floor to accommodate three bedrooms, including the main bedroom, and insert a courtyard at the core of the ground floor plan. Allison had just returned from a trip to South America. "The hotel I stayed in was filled with courtyards. The quality of that soft and subtle lighting was so beautiful. I don't like the idea of having to put lights on during the day," says Allison.

A rough brick wall on the side of the house adds an artistic touch to the living area.

@allisonpyeinteriors
www.pyeinteriors.com
Photos by Jack Shelton

Entrance to Allison's home was previously via a narrow passage to one side of the house. This passage has now been transformed to a slither of a library and, to the rear, a guest powder room, European-style laundry, and a place where coats can be hung. And separating the library from the meeting area where Pye greets clients is a wonderful art nouveau wood-and-glass door, found in a secondhand store. That move transforms the feel of the house, as did the insertion of a new glass front door and side bay window. Allison also installed a woodburning stove and new glazed tiles in the party wall, separating the meeting area from her office directly behind. And while files are concealed behind MDF cabinetry, artwork and objects are beautifully curated on shelves and on her desk and are framed by an endless number of books. One painting that draws one into the house is a large work by Zhong Chen, which Allison often refers to as her "Mona Lisa." "Her eyes tend to follow you, and I often think that she reflects your mood," says Allison. Rather than in a corporate-style meeting area, clients sit at a glass table that's contrasted with a settle, the type of furniture one could find situated near a fireplace in an old English castle.

To separate the studio from the home, there's a large steel-and-glass pivotal door that leads to the open-plan living and dining areas and galley-style kitchen. And linking the two areas is the courtyard, framed by French-style doors on three sides. The courtyard's rendered ivy-clad walls and graphic tiled floor also evoke a South American sensibility. One of the things Susie Leeton advised Allison from the outset was to ensure that the high Victorian-style ceilings were continued to the rear of the home. "The ceiling heights make the spaces feel considerably larger and, of course, lighter," says Allison.

The living room has a casual and relaxed ambience, as does the dining area that's adjacent to the kitchen.

Opposite: The kitchen was designed without overhead cupboards, creating a more streamlined effect.

Courtyards feature prominently in the home, allowing the interior spaces to feel contained.

Opposite: The living area includes a deep, comfortable lounge. The home's spiral staircase forms a neat fit in a relatively tight space adjacent to the living area.

Above left: The spiral staircase takes on a sculptural quality in the home, as well as making the spaces feel connected.

Above right: An upstairs bedroom

Where mission-brown walls and heavily textured carpet previously ruled, the interior bow features off-white walls and wide oak floors throughout the ground floor (except for the pastel-colored tiles in the guest powder room). And most beguiling is the art, with a clever combination of wooden furniture, such as a Georgian sideboard framed with a miniature portrait of two fish dressed in Victorian garb embracing, by artist J. Braithwaite. Another work by artist Janet Laurence brings the outside in with her unique Perspex landscape. The spiral staircase, loosely defining the kitchen, is both sculptural and, importantly, allows for a more efficient use of space.

The new open-plan kitchen and living area now features raw galvanized windows and doors to the rear courtyard, with the doors opening to a raised deck inserted with a singular pear tree. Given the orientation, there was no need for curtains, since high fences on either side eliminate overlooking by neighbors. It's the kitchen / meals area where Allison can often be found, or relaxing on one of her two pale-pink velvet chaises, one of which is framed by a painting by Indigenous artist Sally Gabori. But there's also a sense of artistry with the glass table used as the dining area. Designed by Emanuela Crotti, this table is embedded with a fascinating array of miniature objects, including shells, toy penguins, and other "flotsam and jetsam." Perched above is a pendant light by Ingo Mauro, used by Allison as a photo album as well as a light.

When it came to designing the kitchen, Allison didn't have to consult her clients. She opted for a limestone bench, stained-oak cabinetry, a freestanding Bertazzone oven, and glazed tiles on the wall. The well work and slightly marked leather handles add texture. "These aren't something I would use for clients, as you need a certain personality to accept things that show the ravages of time," says Allison.

Those fortunate to see the bedrooms, including the main bedroom, en suite, and shared bathroom upstairs, will also be impressed. Allison's bedroom is as exquisitely curated with soft pale-pink carpets and a Moorish-style window, providing a backdrop for many objects, the window sourced from a secondhand store. "I love using pink. It's such a soft and calming color, and it's joyful." An ottoman in the image of an apple, designed by leading couturier Maurizio Galante and designer Tal Lancman of Interware, is a delicious addition. And rather than a separate en suite, there's a vanity in the main bedroom, with the shower of the en suite blurred within a tiled alcove around a corner. "You should always buy things you love, things that give you joy," adds Allison.

The main bedroom has a slightly Moorish feel with hues in soft pale pinks.

TIPS

People often overdesign things. I think you should keep things simple and not necessarily notice everything at once when you walk into a space.

    I'm interested in longevity and things that are timeless. But I'm also interested in things that have an element of quirk, or the unexpected.

    I think you should notice the person sitting in a chair rather than the chair.

Opposite: The guest powder room is discreetly located to one side of the home and is accessed via a large steel-and-glass door.

The front rooms are used as the office and are separated by a brick fireplace, thought to be added in the 1970s.

Pye's office is framed with books and magazines.

Art nouveau doors, added in the renovation, add to the home's period charm.

Art, objects, and collections provide inspiration.

TINA ENGELEN

BEYOND FASHION

Sydney, Australia

Interior designer Tina Engelen has a strong idea of where she's headed. She certainly doesn't follow fashion trends and is much more concerned about how a space functions and feels rather than focusing on superfluous decoration. Her approach to design is beautifully captured in her own home, a penthouse apartment in Sydney's Rushcutters Bay, which she shares with her husband, photographer Ross Honeysett.

The couple's apartment, known as the Grid and designed by Engelen Moore, was completed in 2001. Abutting a busy thoroughfare at the front facade but offering a quiet and idyllic aspect to the north with views over Sydney Harbor, both the architecture and the interiors of the one-, two-, and three-bedroom apartments are certainly testimony to having a vision and holding to it. With the lift core of the apartments facing the main strip, the rear elevation is completely opened up with floor-to-ceiling glass doors and generous terraces.

Tina and Ross were previously living with their son Art (now a young adult who has left home) in a 1960s apartment designed by the renowned architect Harry Seidler. However, it was a tad too small, and a move was required. "We didn't really know what that move would look like. It was only when Ian [Moore] and I were presenting the concept for the Grid to our client, the developer, that I was literally seeing how suitable one of the two penthouses would be," says Tina who hasn't changed a thing in her apartment since she and her family moved in over twenty years ago.

www.tinaengelen.com
Photos by Ross Honeysett

The Grid is a landmark building in Sydney's eastern suburbs.

Approximately 1,290 square feet (120 square meters) in area, the apartment features a grid-like plan that includes three bedrooms, a generous open-plan kitchen, and dining and living area, together with a pod at the core that conceals everything from the kitchen pantry and storage on one side, and wet areas such as a separate laundry and bathroom on the other. An internal courtyard adjacent to the main bedroom makes the space feel more like a detached home in the sky than a high-rise apartment on the edge of the city.

The two penthouses share a lobby and a lift, with the green-painted feature wall providing one of the few colors in Tina's fairly monochromatic scheme. Materials are also used in a restrained manner, including an abundant application of terrazzo tiles for the floors, on the island bench in the kitchen, and even on the terrace, including the internal courtyard, which is completely open to the sky. "When we designed these apartments, we approached it like a kit of parts, not dissimilar to LEGO, but of course not with the color," says Tina, who was also keen to create an Australian ambience rather than

Large retractable glass doors create a seamless connection between the indoors and out.

Opposite: The foyer of the apartment features translucent glass walls to allow for privacy for the main bedroom.

pretend the apartment was in New York or London. "It was about framing the views and our unique climate, which has the opportunity of blurring the lines between inside and out."

The kitchen is at the core of the floor plan. The "pod," as it's referred to, features bronze-colored polyurethane cabinetry. However, most of the other surfaces are white, including the Ritek wall (a form of concrete) and the plaster ceilings. There's also an absence of paintings on walls, with the art taking the form of the framed views of the harbor. "It's about light, space, and air," says Tina. The speckled terrazzo is also devoid of color.

Creating a relatively blank canvas allowed Tina to be selective in the type of furnishings she wanted to be surrounded with. One of her choices for the many tan-colored pieces came from the experience of walking through a bank in Milan. "The walls and floor were a pale gray, and all the furniture was tan leather. That interior was already at least twenty years old, but it came with a certain calm and timelessness. It just felt so right," she says.

So, in their apartment, Tina and Ross have the Womb Chair by Knoll, a Square Moore Sofa by Minotta, and the Tate dining chairs by Cappellini, all covered in a tan leather. The Tulip dining table by Saarinen, along with a bedside table, are in Cararra marble. The only other material is the wall-hung Universal 606 shelving system by Dieter Rams. And rather than having feature lights, track lighting is carefully carved into the ceiling. "I prefer not to be distracted with too many objects. Rather than looking at a painting on a wall, I prefer to see the way the light moves and continually changes throughout the day," says Tina, who says the courtyard aspect was inspired by artist James Turrell. The bathroom, including the en suite, is also restrained and follows the palette of materials used in the rest of the apartment, including terrazzo.

"I've never been one to follow fashion. Ross and I are busy, and we don't have time to have things around us that require work and continual maintenance," says Tina, whose home looks as pristine and fresh as when it was first completed over twenty years ago.

An internal courtyard adjacent to the main bedroom makes the apartment feel more like a house.

A minimal aesthetic pervades throughout the apartment.

TIPS

Getting the aspect correct is fundamental. Our apartment is oriented to the north and east, which is something that you can't replace. The free heating from the sun is invaluable, as well as having cross-ventilation.

Focus on the bones of a space and the way it feels before thinking about furniture or other things.

Use a limited palette of materials. I'd like to think that I'm more aligned to fashion designers such as Jill Sanders, using materials sparingly but appropriately.

If a space is well designed, it should also take a variety of furniture and objects. I'd like to think that if someone else moved in here, full of antiques, it would also work.

Simplicity and elegance in the open plan kitchen and living areas

Above right: The en suite bathroom is oriented to capture the light.

Views of Rushcutters Bay continually animate the interior.

The communal swimming pool is like an oasis in the heart of Sydney.

JOHN MARX AND NIKKI BEACH
LOOKING OUT THROUGH MONDRIAN'S WINDOW

San Francisco, USA

John Marx, chief artistic officer for Form4 Architecture, is clearly inspired by early-twentieth-century artist Piet Mondrian. John and his wife, Nikki Beach, both artists, live in this three-level house in San Francisco featuring Mondrian-style windows—rectilinear lines of color like the artist's work. Think of Yves Saint Laurent's Mondrian-style dress in blocks of primary colors. "We bought the house because it had character, was quirky, and [was] bohemian," says John, who didn't want anything generic. Other influences were drawn from Dutch cabinetmaker / architect Gerrit Rietveld for his volumetric composition.

When John purchased the house in the mid-1990s, few were interested. The layout wasn't traditional, spread over three levels, and the main bedroom, for example, was a spacious Californian master suite, with the kitchen being more typical of a galley style one often finds in cities such as New York. Originally built in 1907 in the arts-and-crafts style and added to in the late 1930s, the house was remodeled in stages, initially by creating a garage at ground level. A few years later, the house was almost doubled in size with a three-story contemporary addition.

John and Nikki had lived in the Russian Hill neighborhood of San Francisco since the early 1980s; hence their deep connection to this place—described as dense, urban, and walkable, with more than sixty restaurants and bars within three blocks.

From the moment the couple moved into this house, small improvements were made, including removing rice paper from the wood-and-plaster walls to expose the home's original character—paint was also removed from metal cabinets in the kitchen. But some elements from the more recent past, such as the laminate surfaces in the kitchen and the bold wallpaper in

@form4_architecture
https://form4inc.com
Photos by Bruce Damonte, except where noted

Blocks of color feature prominently in this Mondrian-inspired multilevel house.

Previous page: Photo by John Marx

a small bathroom, circa late 1960s, showing old-fashioned scenes of people carousing in saloons (one of the former owners was a renowned wine writer), were retained.

Since both John and Nikki paint as well as design, the couple's inspiration for the addition to their home came from the De Stijl, where Mondrian was a leading proponent. The duo adopted the art movement's idea of linearity to create dynamic movement—hence everything takes the form of planes and lines, with each level having a portal from past to present—expressed in steel and glass.

While the home's front facade features decorative elements from the arts-and-crafts period, the rear facade features three floors of dichroic glass in primary colors of blue, red, and yellow, akin to Mondrian's distinctive palette of colors. The colors regularly change depending on the time of day,

Color has been strategically placed, both in the selection of furniture and for the stained-glass windows. *Bottom left and right*: Photos by Toni Garbasso

JOHN MARX AND NIKKI BEACH

with the same-colored glass transitioning from red through to purple. To complement the glass, the furnishings on the top level are also deliberately in primary colors.

With the addition, just over 1,400 square feet (130 square meters) was added, taking the form of three large, open rooms. The top level functions as the living room / family room, ditching any formal living area, which is an anomaly to the way both the couple and the broader community in San Francisco live. Not only is the open-plan space ideal for entertaining (there is room for a sit-down dinner for twenty or a cocktail party for thirty-five), but it also doubles as a workspace for John when he's not in the office. As unique is the main bedroom, located on the middle level, which is totally open and leads to a studio—the only doors are to bathrooms.

While the couple took inspiration from Mondrian, with the painted walls extending over three levels, the blue, yellow, and green hues here are not as bright or as overpowering. "We see this more as a subtle homage to Mondrian, more responsive to the hues of a California morning," says Nikki. As colorful are the paintings, objects, and artifacts. An abstract painting by Leslie Andelin spoke to John and relates to his own work.

For John and Nikki, the problem with the original house was that there was "no breathing space." "The place was so cramped that the only way to the kitchen or bathroom was for someone to get up from their seat," says John, who, with Nikki, was looking both for space and natural light. The house now works for a couple, with John sharing his time between the home and office. John generally occupies the top floor while Nikki works on the bottom floor. Both spaces are well lived in both for home and work.

The living / dining area benefits from natural light from one end of the house to the other.

Opposite: Wall-to-wall bookshelves are combined with paintings, drawings, and objects, collected over many years.

While adding a contemporary addition to a period home is always challenging, for this couple the main hurdle was negotiating with the City of San Francisco over building regulations that required light wells, with the result being that a living space had to be sacrificed for light wells. However, some things, with hindsight, would have been done differently, including making the windows more accessible for cleaning—professional cleaners hoisting themselves on bosun chairs is required. But on the plus side, the house now works for an artistic couple who have literally broken through walls and fully embraced a world of color. This house also comes with an impressive list of people who either lived here or visited—including the novelist and historian Charles Caldwell Dobie, followed by Ruth Tieser, a wine writer, and Catherine Harroun, a photographer who was friends with the legendary photographer Ansel Adams, who was one of the many party guests.

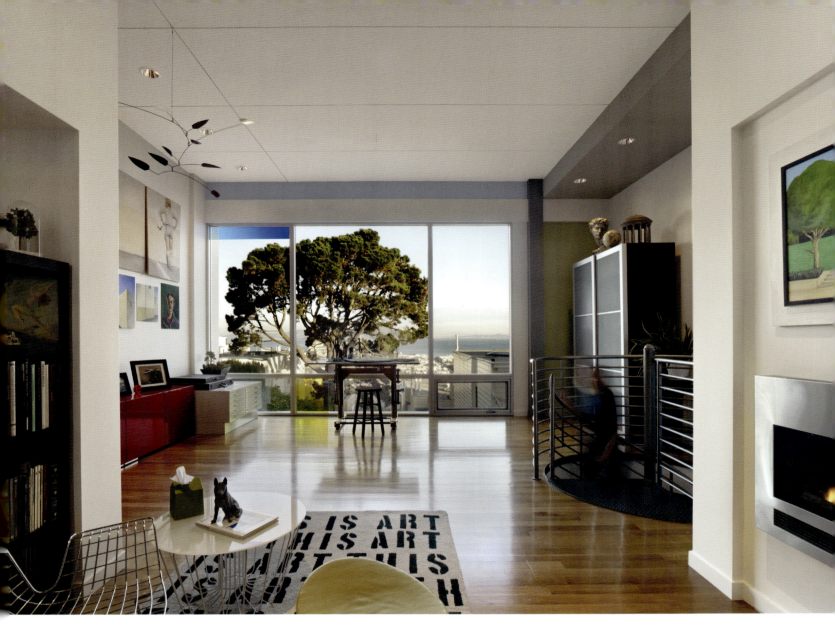

The view over the beach is constantly changing, depending on the time of day and year.

TIPS

Rather than simply move into a new space with mismatched furniture from a previous home, look at new pieces that relate to the new aesthetic or scale.

You need to provide space that will increase the sense of calmness and tranquility. Even in the studio, it's often more empty than full—we always have at least one uncluttered, nonprogrammed flexible space.

Previous spread: Paintings of all dimensions find a place in this home, as do workbenches, which have been positioned for well-lit spaces and views out to the water.

The spiral staircase creates a small footprint in this multilevel home.

ANDREW SHEINMAN
RESPECTING THE PAST

New York, USA

Andrew Sheinman's apartment on the Upper West Side of New York has been home for himself and his wife for the last thirty years. He's the president of Pembrooke & Ives, and this sumptuous apartment beautifully combines the past with the present. "We fell in love with the apartment when we first saw it. It came with such good bones and beautiful detailing. It's like stepping into a different era," says Andrew, who, with his wife, raised two daughters here.

The couple, whose children have left home, were immediately drawn to the area, as are most New Yorkers and those who travel to this highly coveted precinct—including the proximity to Central Park, the Natural History Museum, the Children's Museum, and some of the city's finest schools. "My wife is a fantastic cook, so being so close to some of New York's best food markets was a big bonus," says Andrew.

This apartment has been through several iterations over the decades and has grown and evolved as the family's lives changed. When the two daughters were living at home, for example, they were given the primary and largest bedroom to share, used both for sleeping in as well as to play in. However, when they became young adults and moved out, it was reworked to allow the home to be suitable for a new way of living and for a different phase of their lives. But from the outset, there was always a great respect for the period architecture, which included an original mantel over the fireplace in the formal living area as well as decorative wall and ceiling moldings, together with original wood parquetry floors in most of the rooms. Even some of the original fittings in the bathrooms were retained, such as the distinctive white tiles bordered with black tiles and the 1930s-style basin. "The inspiration for the renovation is largely drawn from Milanese modern interiors," says Andrew, referring to a place and a time (early twentieth century) that he fell in love with on his many travels.

@pembrookeandives
www.pembrookeandives.com
Photos courtesy of Pembrooke & Ives + Genevieve Garruppo

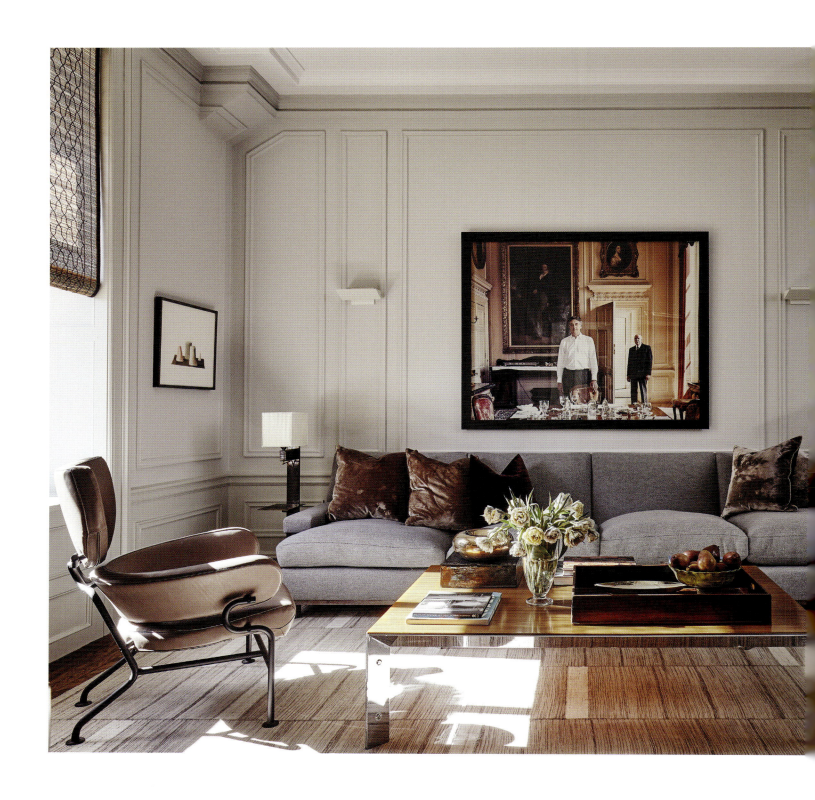

Above and previous page: The main living room in the apartment combines comfortable contemporary furniture with 1950s pieces.

This grand apartment is clearly designed around comfort and for ease of entertaining. There's a fluidity to the arrangement of the spaces, with the kitchen / meals area connecting to the large family room, and its adjacent dining area occupying the center of the floor plan. And while the formal living area features a grand piano and an impressive painting by the renowned artist Cy Twombly, it's the family room that Andrew gravitates to when he gets home at the end of each day to relax in front of the television or read a book. "We've hosted many events in the formal living room, from concerts to cocktail parties," says Andrew, who also likes pointing out to guests that the photograph by Tina Barney above the sofa in the family room is a portrait not of himself but of another gentleman.

Textures play an important role in bringing all parts of the home together. There's a series of neutral color tones such as pale-gray walls that are combined with some of the jewel tones in the furniture and objects. The parquetry floors add a richness to the space, as do the high-gloss lacquered doors, which add a contemporary touch to many of the rooms. There is almost no overhead lighting in most of the living spaces, which creates a more intimate and warm feel to the apartment.

Classical columns frame the living area with rich parquetry floors continuing into the kitchen.

For Andrew and his wife, it was paramount to retain the character and the history of their apartment, because it was one of the main reasons that they fell in love with it. And rather than do a quick makeover, they thought long and hard about each design decision that was made. The art collection has been a lifelong passion, with Andrew first seeing the Cy Twombly work while he was only a teenager. "By the time I was twenty-eight, I was still thinking about it and used all my savings to purchase it. To this day, it sits in the center in my home," says Andrew, who combined such fine-art works with a combination of contemporary and vintage furniture, some of which is postwar Italian. The bathrooms and kitchens were also lightly reworked, with modifications made to the kitchen and pantry areas.

This home feels as though the past is still intact, with much of the original period detailing retained. However, there are also touches of the 1950s, including wall sconces as well as credenzas in the living areas. And although the wet areas such as the kitchen and bathrooms include all the mod cons, there are contemporary layers, such as the extensive built-in bookshelves in the family living area and even in the bathroom. While Pembrooke & Ives is recognized

Left: The galley-style kitchen and breakfast nook benefit from the morning light.

Right: The guest powder room retains many original features.

Above: The library walls are covered with family photos.

Right: The main bedroom has a strong graphic quality.

for its fine interiors, creating one's own home can be challenging even for a designer such as Andrew, whose first commission was to redesign a few hotel rooms in the mid-1980s. "We deliberated over every decision and purchase, wanting to find the right balance of style, comfort, and design," he adds.

A painting by Cy Twombly, *on the right*, is a feature in the living room, as is the grand piano.

TIPS

Restraint is important. It's just as important as everything else in creating the right space. And spaces change, growing and evolving as one's needs change.

People often get the scale wrong. I think this comes from a fear of going too big. But the reality is that going bigger with such things as furniture can often help the room feel larger and more spacious.

Using gloss on areas such as doors can create a more contemporary feel to a room.

If you want to create a sense of intimacy in a room, choose lamps or wall sconces rather than overhead lights.

Left: Cy Twombly on the wall of the living room

Right: A layering of prints and textures from ceramics to books

Opposite: Ornate fireplaces and decorative mantels are combined with armchairs from the 1950s.

The dining room combines classical and contemporary touches.

Wide passages create more-fluid connections between rooms.

Indoor plants and a landscape painting bring a sense of the outdoors into the apartment.

ANDREW PARR

A EUROPEAN SENSIBILITY WITH A CONTEMPORARY TOUCH

Melbourne, Australia

Andrew Parr, one of Australia's leading interior designers, follows his own instincts rather than trends. Although his home in bayside Melbourne is filled with design books and magazines, his large Victorian abode has its own unique personality, with furniture, art, and objects collected over many decades. "When you travel, you pick up ideas and see so many things that inspire you. This house [built in 1880] has a Germanic feel but with Dutch influences," says Andrew, who purchased the house a few years ago with his late husband, Stacey Pablou, responsible for the period-style garden filled with birch trees and oakleaf hydrangeas. With Stacey's niece (who has now moved out) and their dog, Charlie, it was going to be a home for a blended family.

Although this house is large for one person and his dog, there's a sense of intimacy and scale past the front door. In contrast to the home's imposing facade, with its tower, the rooms are bathed in light and soft, delicate, almost pastel tones (apart from the formal rooms at front that feature extensive stained-glass windows). The living room's square bay window is filled with a deep, comfortable lounge and is framed by two table lamps by Pierre Cardin. Here you'll find a combination of styles, including a couple of Pierre Paulin Groovy Chairs from the early 1970s. And in the dining area, separated by original paneled bifold doors, is a glass-top table surrounded by Patricia Urquiola's Bloomy chairs. It's an eclectic arrangement with everything from Fornasetti plates above the fireplace in the dining area, to tribal objects above the marble fireplace in the lounge. "We were fortunate the previous owner did a great deal of the restoration work, transforming what were nine

@_andrewparr
https://sjb.com.au
Photos by Sharyn Cairns and Nicole England

apartments into one house," says Andrew, who took his color palette from some of the deep-burgundy and mauve tiles inset into these fireplaces. Two Italian chandeliers, one in each room, ties both spaces together, as do the room's limed-wood floors.

Other rooms in the house have been thoughtfully reworked to varying degrees. What was previously a formal dining room is now a place for watching television. This benefits not only from soft-mocha-gray-painted walls but also from having unimpeded sight lines through to the swimming pool, enclosed by the former owners but now modified with new windows and doors on two sides to increase the sunlight. Oversized Finnish paper lanterns suspended from the ceiling both in the television area and over the swimming pool further bridge these two areas. "It was all fairly dark, with the timber ceiling over the pool painted in mission brown," says Andrew, who was also keen to link the swimming pool to one of the oldest dwellings on the property, an 1840s wooden cottage that's now used as guest accommodation / cabana room (complete with bathroom).

Previous spread: Large sliding doors connect the pool pavilion to the outdoor terrace. *Photo by Sharyn Cairns*

Above: The pool pavilion feels like an indoor garden. *Photo by Sharyn Cairns*

Opposite: The kitchen and informal meals area are connected to the pool pavilion. *Photo by Nicole England*

The large kitchen also demonstrates the importance of starting with great bones. While the kitchen was previously wall-to-wall brown cabinetry, it's now painted in a French green, including the brown cabinetry. And to give it a more contemporary feel, new marble countertops were included along with a marble backsplash. Large contemporary art by Hazel Dooney in the meals area, along with a 4.9-foot-wide (1.5 meter) plastic pendant light by Vico Magistretti, creates a sense of intimacy but also a soft glow over the table.

Although Andrew let the original house speak to him for direction, he was keen to add things that have meaning to him, reminding him of Stacey or places they visited together. "The exterior of the house is painted a pale pink. You see this color in many Greek towns as well as across southern France. And it just seemed right, rather than the fairly formidable gray or white that's often selected for these period homes," says Andrew, who took some of his color cues from original Victorian schemes. However, there's also a strong dose of the present, including large contemporary artwork by artists such as Adam Cullen that's framed by an Italian chandelier from the early 1970s. A graphic zebra-patterned runner on the stair contrasts with the original wood staircase. "We really didn't buy any new furniture or art for this place. It's been collected over a lifetime," says Andrew.

The kitchen has been lightly remodeled with new painted cabinetry and marble finishes. *Photo by Sharyn Cairns*

Opposite: The entrance to the home features the original doors, left in their original paint color. *Photo by Nicole England*

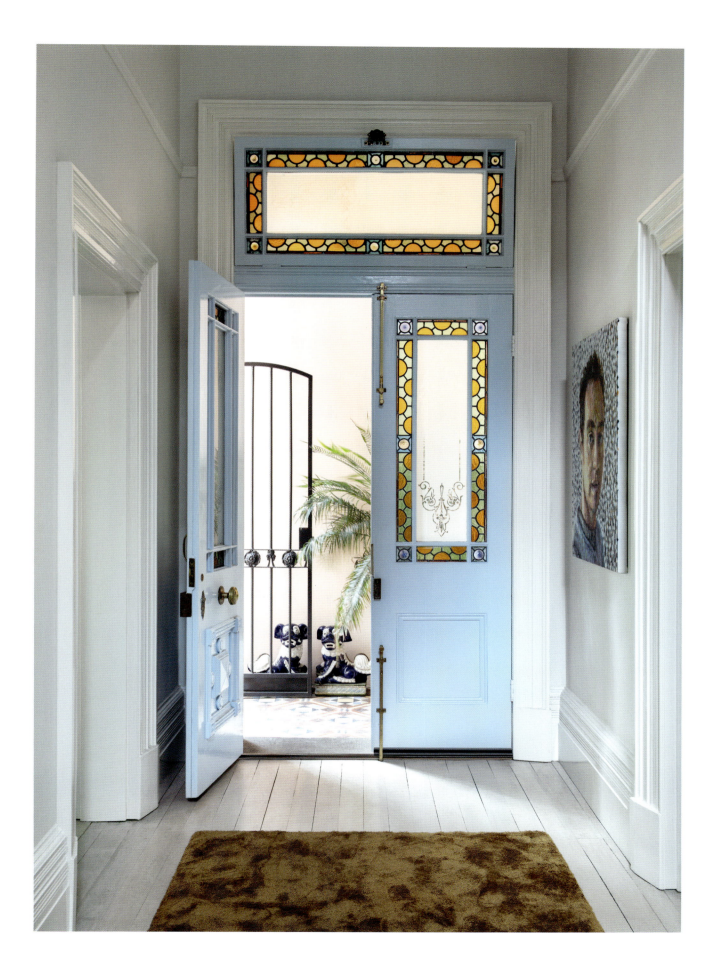

However, Andrew has made a few structural changes, such as transforming what was a bedroom on the first floor into a dressing area that leads from a new en suite bathroom. "I like to retain the DNA of an original room even though it might change its function," says Andrew, who retained the original floorboards and the former cabinetry.

For Andrew, one of the reasons for purchasing a larger house was so that he didn't have to move every time something was done to it. This gives him the opportunity to continually work on the place in stages. He's currently finishing off a hand-painted mural framing the staircase that leads to the tower. Evocative of the Bloomsbury set, it clearly demonstrates that Andrew not only has a finely trained eye when it comes to interior design but also is a gifted artist. "I was fortunate that the previous changes made to this house were sensitively done, saving me the time and expense of redoing things and having to start from scratch."

The formal dining area at the front of the house includes chairs by Patricia Urquiola.
Photo by Sharyn Cairns

Opposite: The formal lounge has an eclectic touch that includes two table lamps from the 1970s designed by Pierre Cardin.
Photos by Sharyn Cairns

TIPS

Let a house speak to you rather than simply imposing your will or what's perceived as the latest fashion. It will tell you how much or how little you really need to do.

It might be tempting to use marble extensively, but there are other and more-economical ways of creating a luxurious feel in a home, whether it's using the right furniture, objects, or lighting, or simply the color scheme that's chosen.

Each room is a different color, but there is a thread that connects the rooms together, whether it's through art, furniture, or variations in color schemes.

An interior should reflect the person or people living in it. At the end of the day, it has to work for them and not simply look great on the pages of a book or magazine.

The lounge also has two 1970s chairs designed by Pierre Paulin.
Photo by Sharyn Cairns

The entrance / stairwell has been carefully restored with a guest powder room tucked under the stairs.
Left: Photo by Nicole England
Right: Photo by Sharyn Cairns

ANDREW PARR

Opposite
Above: The main bedroom and en suite—
the latter converted from a single bedroom

Below: Comfortable lounges and armchairs
make this a home and not simply a showpiece.

Photos by Sharyn Cairns

Photos by Helmut Newton in one of the
living areas. *Photo by Sharyn Cairns*

AESTHETIC

KATE CHALLIS
IMBUED WITH COLOR

Melbourne, Australia

There's no clue as to what's behind this single-fronted 1890s shop front in an inner-city shopping strip in Fitzroy, Melbourne. The transparent glass window with stained glass above conceals a magical home designed by its owner, interior designer Kate Challis. Purchased eighteen years ago by Kate and her husband, Andrew Hallo, who now have a teenage son, Jasper, the shopping strip and the late Victorian building were not what they are today. "There were no cafés, and the area was really quite dreary," says Kate, who could see the potential in both.

Kate lived in this place for fourteen years before making any significant changes. However, when she did, working with Ridolfi Architects, the word quickly got out that something quite amazing lay beyond the front door. What was previously the living room at the front (the place hadn't been used as a shop for some time) was changed to become a kitchen and informal dining area. "As a living area it never really worked. I felt it was too close to the street and required a more intimate feel," says Kate, who flipped the floor plan and located the living area to the rear to receive more sunlight. A garage with a roof garden above it was added, with an exterior circular steel staircase connecting the rear pocket-size courtyard garden to this roof garden, the latter offering impressive views of Melbourne's heritage-listed Exhibition Building, with its distinctive dome.

Less than 13 feet (4 meters) in width, the two-story building includes a central nucleus of amenities: a guest powder room and a large European-style laundry located at the core of the ground floor plan (appearing as a bank of cupboards). Upstairs, separated by the staircase landing is the main bedroom, walk-in dressing area, and en suite on one side, with Jasper's bedroom and bathroom and an additional room on the other.

The living area is oriented to the light well / stair at the rear of the home. Bolts of color, such as for the armchairs, add a sense of drama.

@katechallisinteriors
https://katechallis.com
Photos by Sharyn Cairns

The color palette used for the living area was partially inspired by the artist Margaret Preston.

Given the building's modest dimensions, many would have simply gone for neutral fixtures and finishes. However, Kate is recognized for her adventurous interiors, and considering that this is her own home, she was able to experiment and create an individual vision. The kitchen, with its marble countertop and backsplash, features an artwork by Valerie Sparks called *Le Vol*, which translates to the flight. Birds, with their rich plumage, frame the kitchen bench, the steel bookshelves, and the dining table (designed by Mark Tuckey), with a pendant light designed by Christopher Boots. The kitchen's soft-gray / green cabinetry picks up on the palette of colors in Sparks's art. Coming in directly from the street's pavement is truly an extraordinary experience. "People are generally transfixed when they first enter. It's certainly not expected, both this being a home and, also, fairly adventurous," says Kate, who included stained-oak floors throughout the ground floor and also pushed out a side wall beyond the kitchen to gain an additional 3.3 feet (1 meter) to work with.

The living area, although narrow, has greater depth with the built-in bookshelves.

Lower right: The passage contains a wall of cabinetry, with doors revealing a separate powder room and also a European-style laundry.

Opposite: The kitchen and dining area is now located at the front of the house—immediately behind the shopfront.

Valerie Sparks's *Le Vol* wraps around the entire kitchen and dining area.

While the kitchen and dining area is filled with bird plumages, the stairwell is adorned with Piero Fornasetti's soft-gray cloud wallpaper, with graphic black-and-white-painted stairs in keeping with Fornasetti's graphic style (this combination also highlights each stair tread). However, beyond the staircase, the joyous color can be seen in the living area. Here, Kate took her inspiration from Australian artist Margaret Preston, whose paintings celebrate the rich and vibrant colors found in the Australian bush. Kate retrieves a book showing Preston's work, with one painting of a flowering bush gum placed in a vase. These hues, along with other Australian artists, including a photograph by Jacqui Stockdale of a woman taken partially concealed behind Australian bush legend Ned Kelly's armor, evoke a sense of the native landscape. Fuchsia velvet-covered armchairs in the living area add an extra pop of color, as does a yellow table lamp made from Perspex by UK artist Marianna Kennedy. A dusky-pink-covered chaise complements the room's deep-green walls, a color Kate developed working with Porter's Paints. Other items such as a Fornasetti glass lamp are mixed with a 1970s chandelier. And to increase the light, new steel-and-glass doors were installed to access the garden. Built-in bookshelves frame the space, brimming with books, objects, and artifacts. This cabinetry also conceals a television. "As you can see, I enjoy

KATE CHALLIS   91

Opposite: The dining table is illuminated by a pendant light designed by Christopher Boots.

Above: The passages are enlivened by graphic wallpaper.

Below: The en suite to the main bedroom

creating that element of surprise and contrasting things, whether it's color or periods," says Kate, who likes to combine 1970s glam with contemporary and antique furniture. "I certainly eschew following trends. My clients also want their homes to be unique and for their interiors not to be repeated and seen everywhere," says Kate, who regularly finds unique pieces at auctions or online.

Upstairs, the combination of past and present continues. An Edwardian chandelier greets you at the top of the stairs. And rather than being prescriptive, Kate gave her son the opportunity to choose his own color scheme for his bedroom: a deep emerald green for the walls, and an Aztec-patterned tile for his bathroom. Kate and Andrew's wing on the other side of the first floor is quieter in tone. Their en suite bathroom, for example, features dark walls and a slightly Moroccan feel with its tadelakt floors (a concrete finish). The en suite's feather-like tiles create a wall mural and link back to the bird plumage found in the kitchen and dining area. "Not everything has to be light and bright. You need to have darker and more-reflective spaces as well as areas that offer different experiences," says Kate, whose bedroom leads directly to the roof terrace, with views of the dome of the Exhibition Building, creating a sense of being in Florence.

Left: Dark-painted walls in the main en suite

Right: A small terrace outside the main bedroom

The main bedroom features a palette of soft grays.

TIPS

Don't paint everything in white—that's such an obvious, but also boring, approach.

Create an interior for yourself, not with reselling in mind. You may be in the one house for years, so why not enjoy it?

Don't buy everything from the same shop and at the same time. You don't want your place to appear like a showroom—your tastes change over time, which should be reflected in a space.

Storage is one thing that is regularly underestimated. This place, for example, is quite small (approximately 1,615 square feet [150 square meters]), so you need to include as much storage as possible, not just for now, but going forward.

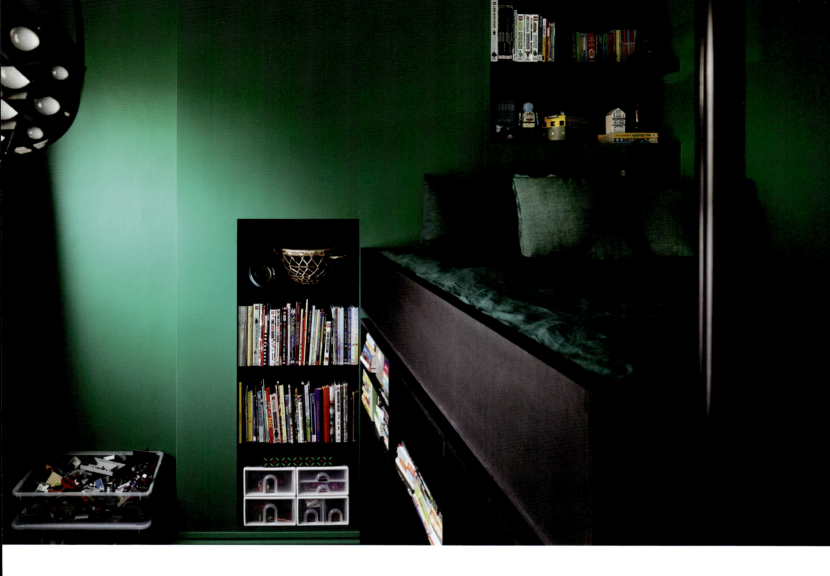

Opposite
Above: The walk-in dressing area adjacent to the main bedroom and a small room at the top of the stairs

Below: The son's en suite bathroom features graphic Aztec-inspired wallpaper, and the bedroom is painted in a deep jewel tone.

Built-in nooks in the son's bedroom increase the sense of space.

SALLY MACKERETH
A COMBO OF JOHN LAUTNER AND DICKENSIAN LONDON

London, United Kingdom

Architect and interior designer Sally Mackereth combined the LA feel of architect John Lautner's inspiration with that of Dickensian London. However, her initial description of her home, which she shares with her two children and two cats, is considerably more complex and intriguing than this comparison. Located in St. Pancras, a five-minute walk from Kings Cross Station, the two Victorian buildings (circa 1870s), one used as her home and the other as her studio, could easily have been demolished, like most on her street from this period.

However, while developers and many others saw the opportunity for a clean slate, Sally could see the opportunity to restore both buildings, but to move them into the twenty-first century. They were initially built as stables for the horses that pulled goods from the nearby canal to the train, and there are numerous hallmarks of the buildings' past that are still clear, such as cobblestones that originally existed in the stables but now form the terrain in the central courtyard that divides home and office, an arched brick enfilade, and even signs of wear and tear, some of which was caused by the horses nibbling away at the bricks, some of which are still blackened by the bitumen. There are even dents alongside the internal steel columns in the home's main living area that indicate where the stable doors for the horses once were.

Most of the original brickwork both for the studio and the house remain, with many of the bricks recycled but used in the same tradition of bricklaying in the Victorian period. "The way the walls are treated is still quite rough, with all their imperfections," says Sally, who had to convince the bricklayers to create that unique English garden bond style with all its imperfections rather than tuck pointing. Above the brick walls is a first floor, with translucent glass walls that allow for privacy and a black steel hood or roof that extends beyond the roofline. And while there are skylights and strategically

These 1970s armchairs by Pierre Paulin are complemented by designer furniture and objects from the 1950s.

@studiomackereth
www.studiomackereth.com
Photos by Henry Bourne

The living areas feature the original exposed-wood beams.

Opposite: Steel-and-glass doors and windows open to a courtyard garden.

placed windows, the large oculus, open to the sky, allows the changing weather to be enjoyed both from first-floor bedrooms and Sally's bathroom and dressing area.

While a breezy LA awaits on the first floor, a darker and considerably moodier ambience can be found at the basement level—where there's a music room and a media room. There's still a connection to the garden at ground level, designed by award-winning landscape designer Christopher Moss. At one end of this middle and ground level are the main bedroom and bathroom (her main dressing area and en suite is on the first floor), with a living area at the core, and a kitchen and dining area at the other. One of the smallest rooms is the television / relaxation nook adjacent to the kitchen, a few steps below to create that sunken 1970s feel, complete with wraparound banquette-style seating. "When I'm lying down, my eyes are aligned with the private garden," says Sally.

In addition to a 65.6-foot-long (20 meter) glass-walled corridor set behind the brick-arched facade, the home includes a combination of contemporary and period features. The kitchen, for example, with its Calacatta Verdi island bench, expressing its deep-green veins, is complemented by large brass drawers below and also a wall of cupboards that literally disappear into a wood-paneled wall, concealing everything from a pantry to kitchen appliances, the latter of which aren't seen unless being used. And in the meals

area, there's an eighteenth-century Belgian wall tapestry, illuminated by a pendant in the form of two glass cherries that add a surreal quality to the space. Two Hollywood chinoiserie chairs, framing the back door to the private garden, also provide a whimsical touch.

Sally pulls her innate style together in the main living area, framed by brick walls and burnished concrete floors, inset with end-grain wood in the center to create that slightly rough and Victorian feel. Here you'll find a couple of Groovy Chairs designed by Pierre Paulin in the 1970s, a Harry Bertoia Bird Lounge Chair from the 1950s, and a chair that completely envelops the sitter, together with a Fornasetti cocktail cabinet, designed in collaboration with Gio Ponti. And for a little humor (not that this house is wanting), there's a rug by Fornasetti showing a snake with a forbidden apple in its mouth. The skeletal-like steel screens, almost whispery in their effect, were found at a flea market in Paris, a number of 1970s umbrella frames stitched together. Linking the home to the studio is a glass pavilion that contains Sally's library, a place where she, along with her cats, can often be found.

An enfilade features steel apertures and cobbled stone pathways.

Right: The home office provides a link to the home and to the commercial office that fronts the street.

Throughout this house, there's the subtle tension between past and present, Victorian versus contemporary. The zigzag, built-in wooden handrail in the oak-treaded staircase is referred to as David Bowie's character Ziggy Stardust, while the palm tree wallpaper in the dressing area is definitely LA—and for a lush and verdant ambience, the terrace below the oculus is heavily potted with ferns. Nothing is predictable in Sally's home. What appears to be a solid brick wall is actually a large pivotal brick door (on a hydraulic system), with the door handle taking the form of a steel brick in the wall! And if a leading designer, who received numerous awards for this house, can't have some fun, then who can! Nothing is predictable, with each space having its own voice and unique character. The front gate / fence with its painted image of an elephant (the street was originally called Elephant's Lane) indicates this is no ordinary house, with many queuing up to take photographs. It's certainly not a John Lautner house from the 1950s, nor is it Dickensian. It's a home that has some elements found in these periods but has clearly moved on to become an intriguing and exciting London home, conveniently located not just to a station but to Sally's studio.

Left: Indoor plants in the dressing area for the main bedroom / en suite

Right: A closer look at the home office, which is lined with books

The main bedroom enjoys vistas into the garden.

TIPS

You need to understand how you live or want to live. There's no point in creating spaces that suit someone else.

You need to understand the context—how a site is oriented and the potential views / outlooks that can be achieved.

When you're looking at your budget, spend money on the touchstone areas, such as handles or the floors. Even if you end up sitting on a wood crate, how much better will this feel if the floors, be they wood, concrete, or covered with a rug, are thoughtfully conceived.

The open-floor kitchen and dining area combines an old tapestry with contemporary furniture.

New steel-and-glass doors lead out of the kitchen to a courtyard.

Opposite: Marble countertops and brass cabinetry feature prominently throughout the kitchen.

The en suite to the main bedroom has graphic tropical-patterned wallpaper, evocative of the 1950s.

Opposite: Echoing the kitchen, the en suite to the main bedroom includes a double marble vanity with twin mirrors, the latter from the 1950s.

TIM VAN STEENBERGEN
A GEM IN ANTWERP

Antwerp, Belgium

Designer Tim Van Steenbergen is well known in Europe as a multitalented figure, sharing his time among fashion, costumes for theater and opera, and ballet products, as well as designing spectacles for Belgium-based company Theo. Interior and product design also features in Tim's extensive design portfolio, with his own art nouveau–style home in Antwerp demonstrating his interior design skills. "There's a thread through all of these disciplines, timeless design based on craftsmanship. It's not about trends but how things are constructed," says Tim. And although he's most recognized for his fashion, Tim enjoys working in the other design fields, with one design discipline influencing the other. "There is always one link through all these areas, particularly with an emphasis on craftsmanship," says Tim, who claims to be really obsessed with people who have craftsmanship, focusing on how things are constructed rather than being distracted by design trends.

Tim's house dates from 1907, part of an early-century building project—with the land once owned by the Nottebhom family, constructing an entire street of elegant and luxurious homes. Sometimes these homes were occupied by the extended Nottebhom family, while at other times they were rented to wealthy German industrialist families who regularly came for business. Tim was well aware of this street before he purchased this house, since it's close to the green quarter, a new green city development in the former military hospital and chapel, the latter now the home of the Jane, one of Antwerp's most acclaimed dining experiences. "This house, which forms part of the Nottebhoms' legacy, is quite remarkable, both individually and as part of an elegant and cohesive streetscape," says Tim.

Tim noticed that one of these houses was for sale, and requested a visit, out of curiosity at that stage. "I was keen to see how these houses were constructed," says Tim, visiting with his partner. They both fell instantly in love with what they saw and brought it as a result.

The main living area is lined with books, both on shelves and arranged on the parquetry floor.

@timvansteenbergen
timvansteenbergen.com
Photos by Tijs Vervecken for Nome Furniture

The living area is "layered" with objects, artifacts, and collections.

Tim appreciated the ability to read the past, with most of the original elements and layout of the rooms remaining—imagining how people in the early twentieth century used these spaces—with the upstairs / downstairs effect. So, when you enter the home via the marble stairs, the formal rooms quickly appear. Alternatively, a few steps below there's a separate set of stairs that lead to the kitchen, where servants would have been busy at work. "Immediately the house is divided into two worlds," says Tim, pointing out the impressive staircase set below the original glass ceiling, which brings light to the two floors below it. There's also a secondary staircase in a second hallway that leads you to the second and third levels, where there's a main bedroom together with the atelier and workshop. The separate layout makes it easier to separate living and work.

In the Antwerp house, there are numerous original features, such as the hardwood floors, ceilings, and fireplaces. All the rooms, including one used as a showroom, are elegantly proportioned with high decorative ceilings and large windows. Tim restored the glass ceiling over the atrium and reinstated the winter garden on the upper level, one of which is now connected to the

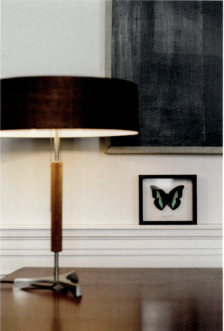

High decorative ceilings bring elegant proportions throughout the home, anchored by a dramatic staircase.

TIM VAN STEENBERGEN

The informal lounge and dining area benefits from a large picture window that frames the back garden.

main bedroom. For Tim, part of the challenge in the restoration process was finding people who truly understood the beauty and importance of the home's original features. "I was always mindful of following the logic of the original plans and structure. When you try to change the structure of the house by, say, adding more corridors or rooms, it tends to feel strange," says Tim, who quickly discovered when moving here that there are few, if any, perfectly straight walls.

Although this is a large house, it allows Tim the opportunity to work and live here without the two colliding. The original structure of the house also made it easy to divide it into a work and living space, one of the initial reasons to buy it. The studio and showroom are situated on the first floor and frame the central staircase, with clients enjoying the pleasure of climbing the grand staircase without going through the more private rooms in the house.

Tim has filled this house with vintage furniture, pieces that show a level of craftsmanship that can also be found in fashion collections. Many of his pieces were found with the assistance of Tijs Vervecken from Nome Furniture. In his main office is a seventeenth-century wall tapestry (a family heirloom)—given to him since he was the only one in the family with a house with large walls. There's also an impressive collection of Belgian postwar modernist paintings by artists such as Guy Vandenbrande and Jan Savereys from the 1950s and '60s that often inspire his clothing. He has also combined these vintage pieces with contemporary items such as the glass coffee table by Gae Aulenti (circa 1980) in the living area, supported by rubber wheels.

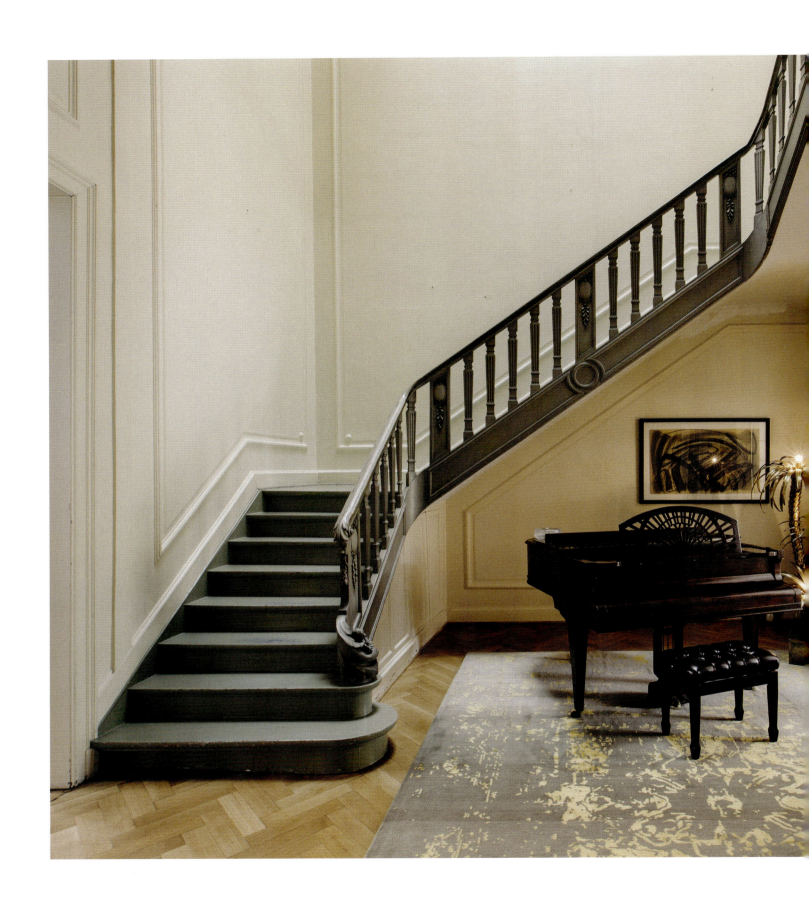

A grand piano fits perfectly as a feature of the main staircase.

Tim Van Steenbergen's office / showroom, located on the first floor

Left: The top level is illuminated by stained glass. Fashion and interiors work together.

Above: A bedroom includes doors on all sides.

In summer, the living area at the back of the house (the former dining room and veranda), which is connected to the garden, is a drawing card and features a large, operable glass door. The private garden, unusual for Antwerp and oriented to the south, is also a pleasure to be in. Tim also enjoys being in the restored kitchen, even though it's located in the basement. "I must have been a servant in a previous life," he adds.

TIPS

Listen to the house and restore it the way it was meant to be—it will be a guide on what seems right or wrong when decorating it.

Craftsmanship, whether it's architecture, interiors, or fashion, requires a full understanding of structure—it's not all about trends, but much more about how things are put together, whether it takes the form of fabric or masonry.

Don't rush things. An interior is a reflection of time going by. It has to be constructed piece by piece, moment by moment.

Don't be afraid of empty spaces!

The main bedroom benefits from a light well.

Opposite
Above: The lower ground floor, containing the kitchen, was originally the servant's quarters—now faithfully restored.

Below: An exam room for Tim's partner, which is also located on the lower level

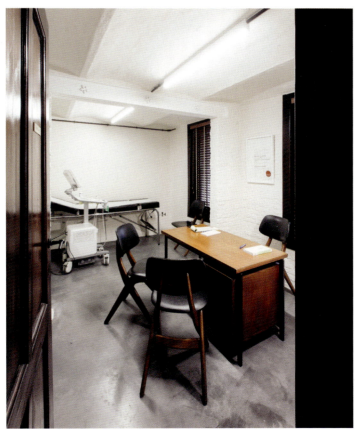

TIM VAN STEENBERGEN

MICHAEL DEL PIERO
MINIMALISM INSIDE A BEAUX ARTS PACKAGE

Chicago, USA

Michael Del Piero, principal and founder of Michael Del Piero Good Design, shares her time between her home in East Hampton, New York, and this small pied-a-terre in Chicago. The latter, featured here, is a collaboration with her Chicago team and allows her to oversee projects in Chicago and the Midwest as well as visit family and friends who live nearby.

While the Chicago one-bedroom apartment is relatively modest in scale, it has been beautifully stitched together, respecting the past of the Beaux Arts architecture of the past while creating a comfortable minimalist contemporary interior. "I'm drawn to good bones, traditional spaces with character. I love working with buildings that have reached their use-by date and giving them a new life—my favorite type of project," says Michael, who appreciated the apartment's rich plaster moldings on the walls and ceiling. And when this sumptuous detail is combined with simple and minimal furnishings and objects, the interior, according to Michael, is allowed to "pop."

This highly curated home has carefully chosen furniture and object d'art that give it its chic sensibility—with only precious objects, including sentimental ones, thoughtfully displayed within a neutral color palette, allowing the many abstract works and sculptural forms to shine and hold court. "It's a relatively small footprint, so everything in it needed to be carefully considered," says Michael.

Although the space captured Michael's imagination on first inspection, she was also attracted to the neighborhood, a mixture of midcentury buildings and classic traditional architecture that frames Lake Michigan. "I certainly appreciated the exterior of the apartment building, which is French in style," says Michael, pointing out the limestone facade with its slate roof and Beaux

Pristine white walls and dark-stained wood floors provide the perfect "blank canvas" for select contemporary pieces.

@michael_del_piero
michaeldelpiero.com
Photos by Aimee Mazzenga

Simple sheer drapes create a light-filled living area.

Earthy and rustic furniture and objects are juxtaposed with the apartment's period detailing.

Arts detailing. In contrast to the exterior, the interior spaces of her apartment needed renovation. Many of the walls were painted in a salmon color (popular in the 1980s), and there was also a series of strange arches that had been added by a former owner. And there was a vanity in the hallway (which now accommodates several black doors to her wardrobe).

The apartment was virtually gutted by Michael and her team, with only the original features such as the acanthus leaf motif on the walls retained. Prior to this renovation, there were also three different types of flooring in the 1,400-square-foot (130 square meter) space. These were completely replaced by a slim board that is more in keeping with the period and is stained an espresso brown. And while the kitchen was always modest in scale, Michael does not claim either to be a great cook or to enjoy the process. "I opted to keep the kitchen quite small (although completely gutted) in order to expand the other rooms, such as the dining room," says Michael. The kitchen is virtually black, allowing it to appear recessive to the adjacent dining area. However, in spite of its size, there's floor-to-ceiling storage on one side and bench height on the other. "You need to create a small space to breathe," adds Michael, referring to the half-white-painted wall in the diminutive kitchen.

The dining area contrasts the more precious, such as the wood furniture, with simple materials such as paper for the lantern suspended over the table.

Bespoke cabinetry in the dining room provides a "container" for glassware and crockery.

Glass-and-steel walls separating the kitchen from the dining area also loosely separate the kitchen. And while Michael has an aversion to cluttering the kitchen, there's a steel-and-glass armoire in the dining area that is brimming with crockery and utensils. "I like displaying some of the more exceptional and unique pieces that I've collected over the years, such as the pewter, silver, glassware, and creamware that I still use for entertaining," says Michael. "They bring back beautiful memories of my life and my travels," she adds.

Michael's renovation was also inspired by the size of the windows and the light streaming through them. While there are various black-and-white shades, there are also subtle hues of caramel and mink, some of which appear in the furniture and objects. And given the size of the apartment, there's a continuity in the materials used—including wood, stone, linen, and cashmere. "All the accessories work in unison, but nothing is too precious," says Michael, who says that "only the weathered, time worn, and soulful make the cut." This includes an original signed lithograph in the living room by Willem de Kooning and an abstract charcoal work by Francine Turk, along with less precious but loved art found at auctions or flea markets. Some objects in the apartment are also treated or presented as art. A Swedish cutting board, for example, is displayed in the entrance as a wall hanging. Likewise, tumbleweed creates a dramatic statement on the living-room wall. It was originally displayed in a friend's home, and Michael convinced her to sell it to her. "She had begged another friend to sell it to her years before!" she adds.

Left: The dining room is simply adorned, with a paper pendant light being a focal point.

Middle: Objects and utensils collected over many years

Right: Less is considerably more in this apartment.

Opposite: The kitchen has been reduced to its key elements—an oven, stovetop, and a sink.

Opposite: The bedroom is a composition of linens and other natural fabrics.

Left: The bedroom has been pared back to the essentials.

Right: With few objects and pieces of art, the bedroom is thoughtfully arranged.

For Michael, this place is considerably smaller than her previous home—a spacious seven-room, three-bedroom condominium. "Downsizing is always a challenge, but so is starting from scratch, with a new kitchen, reworking the bathroom and touching every surface," says Michael, who spends a lot of time in the bedroom, where she felt a softer mood was required. The worn bedspread with its muted okra color envelops the room, and the drapes are lightweight woven cashmere, adding to a sense of luxury. She uses the word "serenity," a buzzword that many designers like to use. "But it's a mood or feeling that's quite difficult to achieve." However, with the subtle use of color and shades, she has successfully created a serene environment.

TIPS

Never use too much of anything, and avoid the superfluous.

I used the Marie Kondo approach—keeping only what brings me joy.

Many people feel that small spaces need small furniture. But I feel that small spaces often require larger items, but fewer of them. The larger pieces make a space seem open and expansive.

Mix modern pieces with traditional furniture, but it's a fine line on what periods work well together. I am certainly not of the school that anything goes. There definitely needs to be a connection, whether it's the colors or materials.

A passage includes generous built-in wardrobes that lead to an en suite bathroom.

Opposite: The en suite bathroom is loosely divided between the bath tub and the "floating" marble vanity.

EMILY GILLIS
PLAYING WITH TONES AND TEXTURES

Melbourne, Australia

When interior designer Emily Gillis inherited this modest 538-square-foot (50 square meter) apartment in South Yarra, Melbourne, it was the location rather than the dwelling that excited her. Previously an investment property for Emily's uncle, the ground floor apartment in a 1960s walk-up had been renovated in the 1990s. So, when Emily moved in toward the end of 2019, she was keen to put her own stamp on it. "The apartment had been rented out for many years, and the few changes made were fairly rudimentary."

Apart from being dated, the kitchen was completely separated from the living area, and there were multiple finishes throughout. The walls, which would have originally been painted white, were now tinged with a faded yellow through the little amount of sunlight that entered, and the different floor coverings made the apartment feel even smaller.

Since the apartment is at ground level and supports the floor above, it wasn't possible to open up the rooms completely. However, small structural modifications can make a significant difference. Emily was able to remove a section of the wall (that was not load bearing) that separated the kitchen from the living area, and was able to insert a marble-clad bench that functions both as the breakfast bar and the main area for dining. The kitchen was also completely reworked with new cabinetry and marble countertops. "When I started this project, I thought it was relatively straightforward; that was, until I was into it," says Emily, who, being on the ground floor with a neighboring apartment block, had to deal both with engaging with the little amount of light available, and privacy.

The living room has a built-in chaise / daybed that extends the entire width of the room.

@emilygillis
www.emilygillis.com.au
Photos by Sean Fennessy

Opposite: Rattan and wood chairs add texture to the living area.

White on white adds a sense of depth to the living room.

Prior to returning to Australia, Emily had been living in a small apartment in Copenhagen, conscious of how the Danes made the most of small spaces. "I grew up in a house, so it took a while adjusting to the change of scale in Denmark," says Emily, who was also captivated by that apartment's simple detailing and light interior.

Given that it is relatively small, every nook and cranny in the South Yarra apartment has been literally put under a microscope. One of the first changes made was installing a built-in window seat that extends the entire width of the living area. While the seat allows for additional guests, the storage below is invaluable. The slim-lined venetian-style blinds were also removed from the living-room window and replaced with a sheer Roman-style blind (this allows for soft diffused light and privacy). The different floor treatments, including carpet and linoleum tiles, were also replaced by an engineered European oak floor in the kitchen and living areas. For the walls, there's now a muro wash (produced by Muro Bond) that includes sand, which adds texture and depth to the once-flat plaster-boarded walls. And the pale-green trims that framed windows and doors were simply removed to create a more streamlined effect.

Against this neutral backdrop, Emily placed a couple of wood and rattan armchairs and a vintage telephone chair; the latter once belonged to her family. A handmade, wooden coffee table by Zachary Frankel was also added. Rather than overstuff the living room, these pieces are thoughtfully combined with a lounge covered by a linen throw. And above this is an embroidered rug, purchased from IKEA, to give the room a handcrafted quality.

Every inch matters in this pint-sized apartment, with the ottomans / stools and the kitchen counter doubling as the dining area.

Simple kitchen shelves create another dimension in the space.

The main and only bedroom has a soft palette, with sheer curtains and a linen bedspread.

Although Emily was able to create more storage in the kitchen, with new MDF painted cabinetry, she was also keen to include some open shelves, ideal for displaying a few personal objects and artifacts. Likewise, the cabinetry in the main and only bedroom was lightly reworked. New doors give the built-in wardrobes a more contemporary feel, and sheer linen curtains allow light to enter, while still providing privacy. The bedside paper lantern further adds to a light and ethereal touch. As with the walls in the living area, those in the bedroom were given a muro wash.

The bathroom, which previously included a tub, was completely reworked. There's now just a shower enclosed with a singular pane of glass. And to replace the cheap tiles, Emily used Moroccan *zellige* tiles, clay tiles made by hand. The uneven surfaces allow light to reflect and, as with the muro wash, add depth to this pint-sized bathroom. And on the floor of the bathroom are cobbled tiles to massage one's feet first thing in the morning. Other additions included changes to the bathroom fittings, such as the unusual lab-style sink—cleverly refashioned from travertine stair treads and reworked by a stonemason. Other details include the bathroom wall sconces by local creative Anna Charlesworth and a new medicine / vanity mirror with a bronze trim.

The bathroom features handmade *zellige* tiles from Morocco and a travertine vanity.

For Emily, this renovation is certainly a case of less is more, as well as her love of combining the past with the present, particularly when it comes to the selection of furniture. "I love playing with different textures, as well as materials that aren't always perfect, almost primitive in some instances," says Emily.

This apartment retains the same footprint. However, unlike the previous state, it's now a simple and elegant home, lived in by a designer who has a truly fine eye for detail.

TIPS

Less is definitely more.

Use materials in a continuous way rather than applying too many finishes and fixtures. Whether it's a house or, as in my case, an apartment, apply an even or consistent approach.

Enjoy mixing different materials and finishes, whether they're a combination of rough or smooth or reflective.

There isn't really a stringent set of rules to follow. But a design should reflect the way you live. I personally prefer interiors that are clean and minimal and feel quite light.

CAROLE WHITING
MINIMAL BUT TEXTURED

Melbourne, Australia

This three-level building in South Melbourne is both home and office for interior designer Carole Whiting. In a gritty urban street, with a combination of showrooms, offices, and warehouses, the building's black-rendered facade with white trim windows can't be missed. When Carole purchased the premises six years ago, it came with blacked-out windows and a history that was a little bit shady (a few deals must have been made; hence the blacked-out windows).

When Carole first saw the three-level, single-fronted pile, she described it as simply ugly. Originally built in 1998 as a combined home and commercial offering at ground level, it had few, if any, redeeming features (except the location). Many of the interior finishes, such as wood floors and cabinetry, featured high-glass epoxy orange. And while most of the walls were white, they had yellowed over time. "I wasn't fazed by any of that. What I saw was that it offered a blank canvas and spaces that would suit both my home and my office. The aspect of the soft morning light was also appealing," says Carole, who lives in the house with her daughter Millie and their two dogs, Scout and Panda.

The studio at ground level, perched above the street pavement, has been reinvigorated by new, pristine white walls, a shade that according to Carole "adapts and responds to creating the right effect irrespective of the natural light." The orange-tinged floors were replaced with limed-oak floors, and on a wall adjacent to the workstations is a painted blackboard wall listing the projects and their time frames. "I like to see what's coming up not just on a day but for the weeks ahead," says Carole, whose methodical and orderly approach can be seen as soon as one passes through the studio's new

Natural textures, such as rattan, timber, and marble, create an earthy quality in this multilevel townhouse.

@carolewhiting
www.carolewhiting.com
Photos by Susan Stitt

The living area, located on the first floor, is connected to a reading nook with a potbelly-style stove.

steel-and-glass doors. Two sets of IKEA shelves frame the entrance, with Carole's signature approach to simple tone and textures (she avoids glossy finishes). Neutral linen curtains both soften the lines and create a subtle delineation to the separate architectural office at the rear (once the single garage). The studio also includes simple furnishings such as an Ercol Love Seat placed in the bay window and artwork by those whom Carole admires, some of whom are friends—Alice Wellinger, August Carpenter, Tom Borgas, and the late and talented artist David Band.

While Carole tries not to mix work with home, she occasionally climbs the stairs to the kitchen and living areas on the first floor when she needs time to contemplate and figure out a few things. As with the studio, this open-plan space has been beautifully curated with an outdoor terrace at one end and a kitchen at the other. And in keeping with the scale of the spaces, most of the art and objects are relatively modest in scale (apart from the overscaled

Right: A bespoke credenza in the dining area adds texture to the interior.

planter placed on the steel grid floor in the internal light well). But on the front terrace, there are generous armchairs designed by Paola Navone where the dogs also gravitate to.

Sitting on the Arflex sofa allows for an unimpeded view both of the freestanding fireplace and the cabinet of curiosities, filled with precious objects and artifacts—everything from Anchor Ceramics to work by the former fashion designer Collette Dinnigan. "Friends tend to know my taste, and they get a feel that I like things and spaces to breathe, in a calm and tranquil environment."

The kitchen is an example of less is more. Previously a composition of glossy orange, wooden cabinetry and marble countertops, it's now a neutral and understated palette—larch wood stained either black or white and large-format porcelain tiles on the central island bench. And to keep things simple, given that everything in the kitchen can be seen from the living areas,

the washing-up area, with its butler's-style sink, occupies one niche, while the cooking area occupies the other. The fridge, freezer, and pantry are concealed, and the stained black wood that frames the appliances in both niches makes the more functional aspects of the kitchen disappear. And while not obvious, some of the fittings such as the fine steel shelf above the sink are in fact traditional bathroom fittings—perfect for hanging the tea towel.

As with the transition from studio to home, there's a subtle delineation between the kitchen and living areas and the bedroom wing, located on the top level. The staircase treads have been painted white. On the top level is the main bedroom (which leads to a terrace), Millie's bedroom, and a bathroom in between. As with the kitchen, everything that can disappear does, such as a built-in pillar adjacent to the bathroom vanity that opens to reveal storage.

The kitchen is pared back to the essentials, with the cabinetry concealing many of the appliances, such as the fridge.

The dining area has been thoughtfully arranged in neutral tones with classic pieces.

The main bedroom on the top level is the perfect retreat at the end of a day.

Carole's bedroom is also exquisitely composed, with the emphasis on neutral textiles, paper lanterns, and linen drapes, one of which conceals a blank plaster wall. "My aesthetic is a cross between Scandinavia and Japan (both cultures know what to highlight and what to conceal)." A bed designed by Ilse Crawford is accompanied by Noguchi paper lamps. "I am drawn to simplicity and craftsmanship, nothing too glossy. And I'd rather be surrounded by fewer things," adds Carole.

Whether it's work or home, there's a sense of calm that resonates through this building, despite its inner-city location, bordered by mixed-use developments.

The bathroom is also restrained and pared back with subtle tones and textures.

TIPS

Wait until you can afford what you really want rather than buying things that you aren't fully happy with—it's really a waste of time and money.

You need to ask yourself how do you want to live, and not be influenced by others and how they think you should live.

There should be a consistency through a place rather than trying to create several looks that tend to fight each other. The spaces will then be more fluid.

The office, a half level above the street, includes a conference table as well as a linen curtain that conceals the workings of the office. A blackboard is continually evolving with new clients wanting Whiting's services.

VICENTE WOLF
WHITE-HOT HELL'S KITCHEN LOFT

New York, USA

Over 3,000 square feet (280 square meters) of living space in New York is a luxury most only dream of. However, for leading interior designer Vicente Wolf, his spacious apartment in a semi-industrial building, dating from the 1920s, is continually evolving as new art and furniture come about. Furniture is also regularly shifted around, giving it another dimension. "It's like making old friends new," says Vicente, who believes that things can't remain static.

Dubbed "the White Knight" for his use of blank slate walls, the walls, floors, and ceilings of his New York loft are all white, creating both a tranquil and calm environment, along with providing a neutral backdrop for his extensive collection of art—including Damien Hirst's *Pharmaceuticals* and a painting by Sidney Nolan, together with objects and artifacts bought on his extensive travels to Asia and the Far East.

However, before laying out any furniture, paintings, or objects in his loft, Vicente wanted to get a feel of the space. "I was attracted to the height of the ceilings and the flow between the rooms—and obviously the amount of natural light each space receives," says Vicente, who prefers a south-facing view that allows his prized indoor plants to flourish.

Hell's Kitchen, which abuts Times Square, appealed to Vicente for its "earthy" character, considerably less pretentious than some other neighborhoods in New York. "There's the good, the bad, and the ugly all living side by side," says Vicente, who was also attracted to the loft's proximity to the Port Authority Bus Station, the area's many ethnic food stores, and the local merchants. But while the neighborhood was alluring, the loft itself was in relatively poor condition, with the floors painted in a bright kelly green. "It was dirty. It took an endless number of hours to bring the place up to its full potential, well

The apartment's white walls, floors, and ceiling provide the perfect backdrop for the many objects and artifacts collected over the years. A bed also doubles as a chaise in the living area.

@vicentewolfdesigns
vicentewolf.com
Photos by Vicente Wolf

before I even moved in and pulling the place together with my vision," says Vicente, who retained many of the original features, including radiators, sprinkler pipes, and the loft's concrete floor.

While there were numerous ideas going through Vicente's mind for how the loft would eventually look, his approach was more to see how things evolved as he acquired various pieces from several sources. However, the loft's bones were the perfect starting point, with their industrial features and wonderful light that comes through the casement windows, common in commercial buildings of the 1920s. The natural light plays off against the white walls, ceilings, and floors.

Vicente's initial concern was for his indoor plants, positioning them in the loft to enable them not only to survive but thrive. His next concern was placing his extensive collection of photographs and seeing where certain items of furniture would be best positioned. He has an affinity for using framed daybeds as sofas. There's a daybed-sofa in the living room, for example, which is a nineteenth-century antique from Borneo, along with other pieces from his remote travels, such as the African Ashanti stool. Situated next to a club-style chair covered in a textured leather, it adds another layer to his loft.

Opposite: Photos and paintings take on a different "voice" when set within a pristine white interior.

Opposite: Large steel-framed windows add to the play of white in this all-white abode.

For Vicente, who dotes on his cat, Micha, the home was not put together with a preconceived objective. Things tended to simply gravitate to a certain space and then moved around to other areas in the loft as his mood dictated. "It's like a party that just blends together," says Vicente, who reupholstered some pieces of furniture, while others were simply left in the state they were bought.

Each space has its own personality, often driven by the artwork that's displayed—collections from Russian avant-garde artists, Italian futurists, and French surrealists, together with American artists and photographers from the late twentieth century. Many of these works are displayed on photo ledges, allowing the pieces to be easily changed. "I feel that if art stays in a static position, one ceases to see and appreciate the work, whether it's visual art or furniture," says Vicente, whose collection of furniture and objects has come from all over the world—Ethiopia, Egypt, Africa, England, Borneo, India, Thailand, Syria, France, and Italy. These items also now have more room to breathe since Vicente opened up a number of the rooms, allowing the spaces to be more fluid. The kitchen was also completely reworked along with the en suite to the main bedroom, after annexing the adjacent apartment.

Although Vicente's loft is large, it has only four rooms, with his bedroom being the place he gravitates to even when not sleeping. He's also attached to his den / guest bedroom / television and exercise room, with his library also doubling as his dining area. And to ensure there's a sense of consistency, the entire apartment is painted in one color, PPG Delicate White, which is also named for Vicente as PPG Vicente Wolf White.

Vicente, who never looks back, only forward, sees some of the mistakes made by people in rushing into making decisions and thinking they can do things themselves. "It's a lot more complex than simply matching up materials or colors," says Vicente, who suggests a furniture plan from the outset, seeing how items will appear on paper in terms of scale, before any purchase is made.

TIPS

Always trust your gut. It usually provides the best answers.

Separate your collections around the home by creating tableaus to give them meaning.

Opposite: There are points of interest in every space, including artifacts from Southeast Asia.

A Danish classic from the 1950s is the perfect place to unwind at the end of the day.

Above: The main bedroom features a sleigh-style bed and generous armchairs for reading.

Left: Even chairs provide the perfect prop to display art.

Opposite: An antique side table has been transformed into a vanity in the bathroom.

FUNCTION

DOROTHY MEASER

URBAN PASTORAL HOUSE

Los Angeles, USA

Interior designer Dorothy Measer, director of dk designhouse, found it challenging buying a house that offered a sense of a rural environment but was close to all the amenities found in the city. With her husband, David, and now with two teenage children, they had always entertained the idea of having a house in the country, one that would, according to Dorothy, "engender a slower lifestyle, surrounded by nature and animals." When they realized that the ideal property didn't exist, they set about creating an urban home in Venice Beach. One that felt pastoral.

Located at the junction of two relatively busy streets in the Mar Vista neighborhood of Los Angeles, not far from Venice Beach, the couple's home—a two-story house with a high front fence and a verdant, almost wild garden—was designed with low-water native Californian meadow grasses, succulents, and grevillea trees, the latter acting as a barrier to the traffic. "There's a vibrant energy here, quite urban and gritty," says Dorothy, who saw this location, at the crossroads of two neighborhoods, as offering the possibility for experimentation and creativity. And although this wasn't the country, there was sufficient space on the corner block to have chickens.

From the outset, the couple's vision was for a new two-story house that brought together urban / rural and blurred the divisions between indoors and outdoors, formal and casual areas, and public and private, much like the location itself. "I was inspired to integrate and juxtapose rural and natural elements into the best aspects of urban life. From farm-to-table restaurants to glamping to farm markets," says Dorothy, who wanted this urban space to be

dkdesignhouse.com
Photos by John Ellis

Previous spread: Coastal planting creates a thriving and low-maintenance garden.

Above: The swimming / plunge pool on the edge of the main living space

Left and opposite: Curves feature extensively, from the main staircase to the bespoke island bench and cabinetry in the kitchen.

experienced through the lens of nature. This was achieved by the verdant outdoor green space that frames the house, dotted with fruit trees, an outdoor fireplace, and an outdoor dining / lounge area that includes a thriving vegetable garden attended by David. The heavily planted green roof also extends the vegetation, further concealing streetlights and power lines. Dorothy worked closely with landscape designer Eddie Martinez, director of Ed's Landscaping.

While the indoors and outdoors blur, the family tends to gather in the kitchen, which flows into the living and dining areas. Dorothy used a Swiss perforated wood to create the kitchen island bench, along with a series of engineered screens throughout the house that create a moiré effect that evolves during the day—creating a lantern effect at night. These cylinders cleverly conceal back-of-house functions such as a powder room, A/V equipment, a pantry, and a bar. The sculptural island bench in the kitchen manipulates the perforated wood shape from convex to concave and encases vital functions, including space for bench seating for casual meals and looking on while one of them prepares a meal. Dorothy also included curved bookshelves that delineate bedrooms on the first floor. Radiating off this library are a home office, balcony access, and three bedrooms with en suite bathrooms. And as with the ground level, there's greenery on the first-floor landings, assisted by large picture windows.

The dining area benefits from the coastal breezes.

In keeping with Dorothy's vision to green a patch in an urban context, she used a variety of soft neutral and mossy greens to connect to the plants. A combination of European species and finds from local vintage stores can be found in the living area. "This patterned rug and whimsical wooden side table hint at stylized nature," says Dorothy, who also chose local established and emerging artists to display in her home—including Lynn Hanson, John Baldessari, Edward Ruscha, and Elissa Levy.

For Dorothy, it felt like a luxury to design a completely new house rather than remodel an older home. "It allows you greater freedom to create spaces exactly as you like them, not having to compromise." However, one of the largest challenges pushed not only Dorothy but also the builder and carpenter out of their comfort zone—and that was creating the serpentine stair that intertwined between translucent columns. "I feel indebted to their talent, skill, and persistence that made these elements come to life," adds Dorothy.

The dining area is as imbued with the feeling of nature, appearing as an enchanted forest—with its steel-based dining table applied with countless layers of enamel to give it the depth of a mottled mossy floor. Green vintage Gaetano Pesce chairs also pick up on the garden theme, as does a unique pendant light over the dining table that connects to local flora with its bronzed-iron oak leaves (native oaks are a protected species in California). The branches of this light shower dappled light of delicate shadows of the leaves on the tabletop. And what could be more soothing than looking out to the yard filled with meadow grasses and a solitary orange tree, another nod to California.

Left and following pages: The curvaceous staircase makes its presence felt on every level.

The living areas at ground level have a casual and informal ambience.

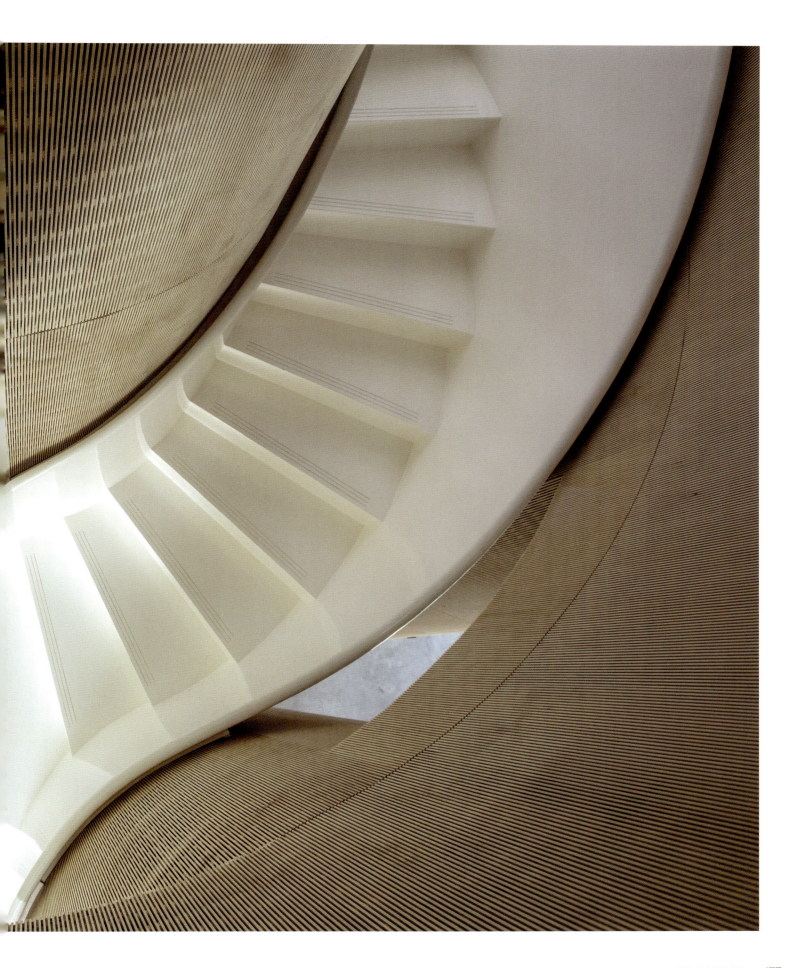

Even the built-in bookshelves are curved.

While the kitchen is a focal point for the family, the en suite to the main bedroom is a well-earned reward for Dorothy at the end of a day. It was inspired by friends who moved to the Philippines who had a spa in their bathroom that also merged with the walk-in dressing area. "That inspired me to include a lounge area in ours, combining the dressing area with the bathroom."

This is certainly not a country house, nor is it strictly a hard-edged urban townhouse. Combining the two makes this home unique.

TIPS

I think that the old rule that my mother's generation applied to dressing should be applied to spatial planning within a home. The idea that you should look in the mirror before leaving the house and remove one piece of jewelry is a good thing to consider when designing a home. Sometimes, just removing an item or two from a room can make a large impact. Sometimes, that piece of furniture can simply be moved to another room. Or try swapping one piece from another space.

Take a risk and try adding an element that is out of your usual comfort zone—maybe an unusual plant, a wall hanging, or a vintage lamp—all achieved with a very small financial cost. Each element plays a role in how the space works and feels. Experimenting this way can have a larger impact than people imagine.

Slate-gray-tiled walls and bespoke cabinetry in an en suite

The main bedroom and en suite are imbued with soft tones and texture, such as the unusual tiled floor in the bathroom.

B.E ARCHITECTURE
TREATED LIKE A HOUSE RATHER THAN AN APARTMENT

Melbourne, Australia

These 1960s apartments in a leafy boulevard in the Melbourne suburb of Toorak were thoughtfully designed by Perrot Lyon Mathieson. The cream-brick apartments are surrounded by gardens and are oriented to the north, with access via south-facing doors from a landing. Most of these apartments are still in fairly original condition. However, this one has been completely reworked, treated like a house renovation rather than something that's more transitory.

The owners, two leading designers, were aware of this apartment block well before the couple purchased it. "It certainly wasn't a difficult decision to buy it, given its position, its orientation, and, importantly, the way these apartments are planned. One of the first things that initially caught our eye was the eighty-year-old camphor laurel," say the owners.

Although quite modest in scale, approximately 1,300 square feet (120 square meters), the apartment feels considerably larger and is sumptuously appointed. What was a three-bedroom dwelling is now two bedrooms, with the second bedroom used as an office by one of the owners and by the much-loved cat Pud's bedroom. With a bank of built-in cupboards, it's also used as a second dressing area (her clothes are in the main bedroom). "When we first moved in, there were three bedrooms (one in what's now the kitchen), but there was really only a need for two," says one of the owners, who could see that the place came with great bones, including a brick skin (walls) and a concrete floor that allows for acoustic separation between apartments. However, new double-glazed windows were installed, both to reduce the sound from any passing traffic and, importantly, for thermal insulation.

@b.e_architecture
www.bearchitecture.com
Photos by Felix Mooneeram

The living area enjoys generous light throughout the day.

The faux wood floors above the concrete were removed and replaced with terrazzo tiles, and many of the walls, excluding the kitchen and bathroom, were lined with Japanese grass wallpaper, popular in the 1950s and '60s. "We can honestly say that there's not one plaster wall in the entire place," she says. Since the apartment was literally taken back to its bones, every detail could be addressed, whether it was increasing the size of doorways or using brass for floor skirtings or edging on bookshelves. "The palette is quite simple, but the material palette used extends to every room," he adds.

The living room, leading to a north-facing terrace, is beautifully appointed with furniture and art, with contemporary pieces combined with antiques. An Attola glass lamp from the 1960s on a Biederermeier table speaks to a plastic floor lamp by Kartel. Two large armchairs designed by Gio Ponti from the 1950s are draped in Tibetan lambskin. The large module lounge, almost 13 feet (4 meters) in length, is also regularly covered, since the furniture is a tempting scratching pole for Pud. A triptych by artist Pat Brassington is placed opposite a portrait of a Spanish woman painted in the eighteenth century and placed in an ornate gold frame. And to ensure that the dining and living areas read as one, there's a Saarinen Tulip table framed by Japanese-style cabinetry, made from felt and wood. A bronze mirror inset in this cabinetry reflects the verdant outlook.

Brass detailing adds a special edge to the room.

A triptych by Pat Brassington is a feature in the open-plan living and dining area.

B.E ARCHITECTURE

Unlike many homes today, where open-plan kitchens and living areas are the norm, this kitchen is fully enclosed. Finished with wood veneer cabinetry and tundra-gray marble countertops and backsplashes, it gives the couple a degree of privacy when preparing meals for friends. And to ensure privacy from neighbors using the outdoor landing, opaque glass was added above the kitchen sink.

Unlike many apartments, particularly new high-rise ones where bedrooms are relatively modest in size, this one is generous. How often would one see a baby grand piano in a bedroom? It's also used to display Japanese artifacts. There's also a print on the wall by Michelangelo, something that the owner has carried with him, like the piano, from his childhood. And while there wasn't sufficient room for a separate laundry, given the width of the passages, there was enough space to include a European-style laundry, concealed behind wood veneer doors.

The dining area has built-in cabinetry and raffia wallpaper, a paper that was popular both in the postwar period and now.

Opposite: The kitchen was completely reworked to allow for additional storage.

The main bedroom also accommodates the piano.

The bathroom was completely reworked by the couple, with terrazzo-tiled floors and walls. Even the vanity is made from Fallow stone, with a basin appearing to have been carved into the vanity. And given that it's only a couple living here, there's an open shower that makes the bathroom feel considerably larger. Rearranging this area also allowed for a generous 6.2-foot-long (1.9 meter) bath to be included in the renovation.

While the couple regularly travel, they enjoy coming home. They see their apartment not just as a place to live in between trips, but a place that feels like a house. "We didn't just do a quick makeover. Everything here is designed for the long term, with apartment living more attuned to the European psyche," he adds.

Terrazzo features prominently in the apartment, with brass detailing at every turn.

The entrance has been slightly partitioned to create a sense of arrival.

Raffia wallpaper complements the 1960s lampshade.

Opposite: The en suite bathroom was completely reworked.

TIPS

There's certainly more than one approach to doing something. But our approach is to do something well and for the long term rather than for a short transitory stay.

We were after a European-style apartment, one that was quite layered and would provide a backdrop for the art and objects we treasure.

You don't have to compromise when you're designing for yourself.

Don't follow fads or passing fashion, and be consistent in the way you handle things.

THOMAS GEERLINGS
CANAL HOUSE

Amsterdam, the Netherlands

This five-level house on a canal in Amsterdam, circa 1896, is set behind a warehouse facade. Relatively narrow in width, the home of interior designer Thomas Geerlings, his wife, Danielle, and their two children offers surprises at every turn. He was the founder of Framework Studio, and the house is beautifully curated with fine objects, contemporary furniture, and lighting. "I bought this house primarily because of the location. As an interior designer, it's one of the few things that I can't possibly change," says Thomas, who, in his opinion, sees it as one of the most coveted inner-city streets in Amsterdam—close to the Amstelveld Square in the historic part of the city and within a UNESCO heritage-listed location.

While some discover problems with an older house only once they move in, Thomas says that from the outset, "I bought a ruin," and one that occupied a footprint of only 538 square feet (50 square meters)—without any garden. "There was really nothing redeeming about the building. Everything that we touched fell apart, with most of the timber having rotted," says Thomas, who literally gutted the building. Although the place was devoid of period detailing, given its original function as a warehouse (most of this past was removed), Thomas took his inspiration for this original use as a storage / warehouse facility—selecting rough materials and exposing the few rough remnants, such as peeling back the paint from the original beams and ceilings. "Amsterdam's rough and rural periods inspired me. These warehouses were considerably darker and less sophisticated than many of the fine homes built along the canals. There was huge wealth in this city, but there was also extreme poverty and devastation," he says.

With two children, the couple could have opted for a low-maintenance, robust house where the children could play indoors (since there's no garden). But he thought that by creating beautiful spaces filled with art and objects,

Paring back a room to its essentials, a comfortable chair and an open fireplace in the living area

@*frmwrkstudio*
www.framework.eu
Photos by Kasia Gtakowska

Views of the canal through the home's generous picture windows

The living area features wood floors and built-in rattan cabinetry.

their children could learn to appreciate art—value it by living with and respecting it. So, unlike many children's rooms that have a special aesthetic—fun, colorful, and, importantly, not overly precious—here you'll find ceramic lights on the ceiling; beautiful oak cabinets; sculptural, velvet-covered headboards; and various art pieces.

Thomas also used a similar palette throughout the house, whether it was for the children's bedrooms, the dining and living areas, or in the kitchen. Cement-rendered walls, raw finishes juxtaposed with fine steel-and-glass vitrines, together with a muted green / gray color palette, appear throughout. Thomas was channeling a brutalist backdrop in keeping with the origins of the building. The kitchen, which features gray marble countertops and backsplashes, also includes a graphic white screen with an abstract green pattern that provides a sense of the outdoors, given that there's none to be had. A new steel-and-glass skylight over the kitchen / meals area also brings in a sense of the outdoors, with its strong connection to the sky.

The first floor, used as a living area, features a long, continuous bench along one wall, where both adults and children can either work or simply spread out papers or books. "I can easily distill my approach to a few words—green, cement, light and art," says Thomas, who was as careful in selecting the works of art and furnishings for his home—a combination of furniture designed by Framework Studio and paintings by Lamberto Teotino, Iris Schomaker, Jan Schoonhoven, Cecilia de Val, Parrick Grijalvo, Stan van Steendam, Dirk van der Kooij, and Martin van Wordragen, just to name a few. The lights, including those by Achille Castiglioni, add a gentle glow to the spaces, while a rocking horse by Stevensons Brothers adds a more whimsical side to the design. The glass cabinet / Wunderkammer by Piero Lissoni adds a slightly museum-like quality to the home, but instead of antiquities, it is filled with additional towels and linen that can be accessed by the adjacent bathroom.

The narrow home appears considerably wider with its bespoke furniture, including a bench seat that extends the entire length of the room.

Opposite: The kitchen is almost "sculpted" out of the space, with tiered beams adding depth to the walls and ceiling.

A large skylight / roof above the kitchen and dining area brings light into the core of the home.

For Thomas, who is used to making spaces feel considerably larger, this home perfectly exemplifies his ability to transform even the smallest footprint into a magical home for a family. However, while the spaces are modest, they benefit from the extended views of the canal, with the living room on the first floor enjoying one of its prized water views. "Most evenings, you'll find us around the kitchen table, either with family or with friends," says Thomas.

TIPS

People often think that they can adjust parts of a house by themselves. You cannot do it without having the skills and experience.

A design, irrespective of an aesthetic, has to have coherence, since every space is connected, even though in this case there are several levels.

You can't simply remove a few items and replace them in a piecemeal way. It might seem cheeky, but "a car does not drive on three wheels and a banana!"

Bespoke wooden shelves complement the chunky beams that traverse the ceiling.

Opposite
Top left: Chunky beams add texture and depth to a modest-sized bedroom.

Top right: Soft muted tones create a sense of calm.

Bottom right: The main bedroom includes a sleek glass vitrine that functions as a wardrobe.

Opposite: Given the width of the house, the staircase is reasonably narrow by today's standards.

One of the children's bedrooms features bright and poppy furniture and art, including a sculpture of a dog that doubles as a seat.

MELISSA DE CAMPO
A SKI RETREAT

Victoria, Australia

A four-hour drive from Melbourne, this ski lodge in Victoria's high country offers a completely different environment for interior designer Melissa de Campo. Founder of Design Consigned, a business that specializes in high-end designer vintage furniture, lighting, objects, and art, Melissa enjoys being in her apartment during her downtime. Originally built in the 1990s, Melissa purchased this place twenty-five years ago, enjoying raising her children there when they were young. "We spent time snowboarding [Melissa still enjoys this activity], and I'm still captivated by the spectacular views over the snow runs, from dawn to dusk," says Melissa.

One of five apartments in the ski lodge, Melissa's three-bedroom home is designed over five split levels. At the lower levels are the garage and mudroom, with the ground level given over to three bedrooms and a bathroom (originally for the children or guests). And on the middle level, where Melissa spends most of her time, is the open-plan kitchen, dining area, and living area, with the Apres bar in the kitchen where most gather after removing their skis. And on the top level is the main bedroom, with a large en suite.

An American Rocky Mountain feel predominates, with wood paneling, exposed Oregon beams and numerous objects and artifacts sourced from travels, particularly through European ski villages. The apartment is quite woody, not surprisingly, given that the original owner of this apartment was a timber merchant. The wood, including the built-in kitchen cabinetry, is framed by stone walls or, alternatively, tongue-and-groove walls.

@designconsigned.com.au
designconsigned.com.au
Photos by Melissa de Campo

Comfortable rustic-style leather furniture was selected for the main living area.

The home's exposed-stone walls and chunky wood rafters add warmth to the place.

Bottom right: Maarten Bass's Smoke Armchair for Moooi is a feature in a corner of the living area.

The Favella Chair by the Campana Brothers would make for extremely costly firewood.

While Melissa appreciates the extensive use of wood (the owner also left behind a large, chunky, wooden dining table), she was keen to create a slightly lighter and more European ambience. So, while the kitchen cabinetry remains, it's now complemented by a glossy, black-tiled backsplash. And in the dining area, there's now a more slim-lined table accompanied by banquette seating. As soon as Melissa arrives, she gravitates to the fireplace in the main living area and sits in one of the three comfy leather lounges. An armoire from France, with its chicken-wire doors, displays some of the artifacts collected over many years. The furniture is just as contemporary as it is rustic, such as a black smoked armchair by Maarten Baas for Moooi and a Favela chair by the Campana brothers for Edra. Other pieces include a bronze sculpture by Australian artist Dean Bowen and a black AJ floor lamp by Arne Jacobsen for Louis Poulsen. French-style wall sconces emit a soft and warm glow in the space, something that's often missing in many chalets built today. "I have an aversion to sharp and intense lighting, such as spotlights. They just don't seem to work in these environments," says Melissa.

There's a mélange of furnishings and objects here. While they appear randomly placed, they have been carefully curated with a designer's eye. "I love primitive art, tribal pieces, whether from the Eskimos or from the American Indians or from Southeast Asia, showing the diversity of our world," says Melissa, who also found a couple of vintage wicker chairs from the 1930s on the roadside that are now on the balcony adjacent to the living area.

Cold days are as appreciated, whether this means spending time in the cedar-lined sauna a half level above the living area, or under the covers in the main bedroom, located on the top floor. Trophy mounts adorn the wooden wall above the bed, often the place where her dog can be found.

While Melissa spends most of her time living in her inner-city apartment, she loves the regular escape to the snowfields. "I call this my happy place, a place that allows me to completely unwind." The many objects found here also rekindle memories of all those trips traveling abroad to small ski villages and other places such as Argentina, where even the smallest items, such as a little silver trinket box placed on her bedside table, remind her of the places where she bought them.

Right: The en suite to the main bedroom includes a large soaking tub.

Melissa refers to her design approach as Alpine Primitive, things that are rarely seen at home, such as her pigskin Mexican bar stools adjacent to the Apres bar. "I love the patina of the leather. It just gets better with age, even if they are forty years old," says Melissa, who also enjoys the fact that she could be anywhere here. Orchards, for example, can often be seen in the apartment, something that's rarely expected in a snow environment. "And of course, I love mixing things up, the old with the new," adds Melissa.

TIPS

Lighting, particularly in this environment, should be soft and quite moody; for example, the ball-shaped light made from reeds above the French armoire in the living area. It's about creating a sense of warmth, even if there is a blizzard outside.

Instead of purchasing thirty souvenirs while traveling, get just one thing that resonates, has meaning, and will continually remind you of that special trip. Be prepared to dig a little when you enter a store. It might not be obvious at first, but you'll know that it's right when you finally discover it, often in the back of a store.

Some items, such as de Campo's fur-clad wallet, are used only while I am staying at this apartment—that gives me the sense of being in a different place.

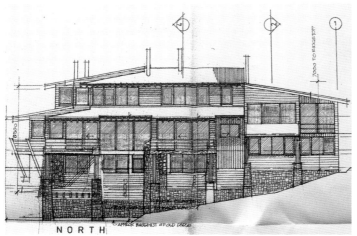
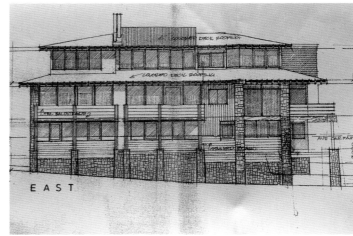

NORTH

EAST

Opposite: Elevation drawings of the multiunit lodge built in the 1990s

MELISSA DE CAMPO

CANDACE BARNES
VIEWS FROM THE TOP

San Francisco, USA

Interior designer Candace Barnes is fortunate to live in a penthouse apartment in Nob Hill, San Francisco. From every window there are impressive views of the city skyline. "We were looking for a certain amount of space in a preeminent location, something that would afford us everything we wanted and more," says Candace, director of Candace Barnes Design, who lives here with her partner.

Candace has lived in San Francisco for decades, and this location not only was in the center of the city but came with downtown views, wonderful restaurants, and great architecture. Her penthouse, named the Chambord, is included in many of the city's walking and architecture tours, as is the neighborhood itself, which is well endowed with architectural gems. The Chambord, built in 1921, was designed by James Francis Dunn and features several Beaux Arts influences. "People walking by often think that it was designed by Antonio Gaudi," says Candace, pointing out the rich and fluid detailing on the exterior of these distinctive apartments.

When Candace entered the penthouse for the first time, she was captivated not only by the impressive views but also by the spaces. She knew that there was some superficial remodeling that needed to be removed, restoring it to its original condition while still giving the place a contemporary feel. Fortunately, the penthouse came with high decorative plaster ceilings, Solomonic columns, marble and inlaid parquet floors, an oval-shaped dining room, open fireplaces, and even a concealed art deco bar. This ceiling was partially concealed with a series of strange midcentury paneled lights (fourteen in total) that had been added in the 1950s. "There was also some sort of an alter niche in the main living area, which had to go," says Candace, who recalls the weight of this concrete and plaster niche, estimated to be in the hundreds of pounds. "Of course, everything in remodeling becomes greater than you anticipate," she adds.

Spacious, light-filled rooms and period detailing add to the charm of this historic apartment.

www.candacebarnes.com
Photos by Patrick Argast

Candace wasn't particularly inspired by any artist or designer for this renovation. However, the library, with its grand fireplace, bookshelves, and hidden niches in the paneling, did lend itself to a certain color scheme—a classic Billy Baldwin, chocolate brown with crisp white trims. "I recalled from long ago that this was a color scheme that he used. I also had two original Michael Taylor sofas from the 1950s craned in past six stories through French-style doors in the dining room," says Candace, who breathed in, noticing that there was not an inch to spare between these doors.

Since Candace enjoys entertaining with friends and family, she was keen to create fluid spaces and take advantage of the 360-degree views offered in every room. And, given that the couple occupies the crown of the building, they benefit from the natural light. While the apartment is firmly embedded in San Francisco, it has a distinctive French ambience, with generous ceiling heights and small-paned windows that add to the home's European ambience. Color and texture are a strong focus for Candace, as well as combining contemporary furniture with antique pieces. Candace is also an antique dealer and formerly had a large, 4,000-square-foot (372 square meter) showroom in the city's design center. While there are a few antiques to be found in her apartment, many of the pieces, such as the dining-room table and chairs, along with the grand-scale, glass-topped iron console table, were designed by Candace. Other features include a tactile wall covering in the living room that takes on the appearance of snakeskin.

While interiors are obviously important for Candace, so are the outlooks from windows, whether it's her own home or from those in a client's abode. From the entire length of her penthouse apartment, there are views of Grace Cathedral, an iconic landmark in San Francisco. The home office and main bedroom also benefit from a postcard view of the city, while the western aspect is toward the ocean. "I love reading in my library, next to a roaring fire," says Candace, who also enjoys sitting on the balcony adjacent to the living room on warmer days. "The cathedral bells are a continual reminder of where you are," she adds.

For Candace, her fine eye comes with editing, knowing what to put in as much as what to leave out of a space. "I know when I need to stop," says Candace, who understands aesthetics as much as creating functional spaces.

Decorative ceilings and a period fireplace are juxtaposed with 1930s-style club armchairs.

Opposite: The living area has impressive views of Grace Cathedral.

Embossed wallpaper and a chandelier add a touch of glam.

Following spread: The main bedroom includes an open fireplace and stained-glass windows.

TIPS

Don't use a console table when you really need drawers or a cabinet in a space.

Utilize pairs, whether it takes the form of furniture or objects, and pay attention to spatial relationships.

Large items in small spaces are powerful.

Create flow and continuity between rooms by repeating colors or textures from room to room.

Always think vertically. So much space can be created visually above us in a room.

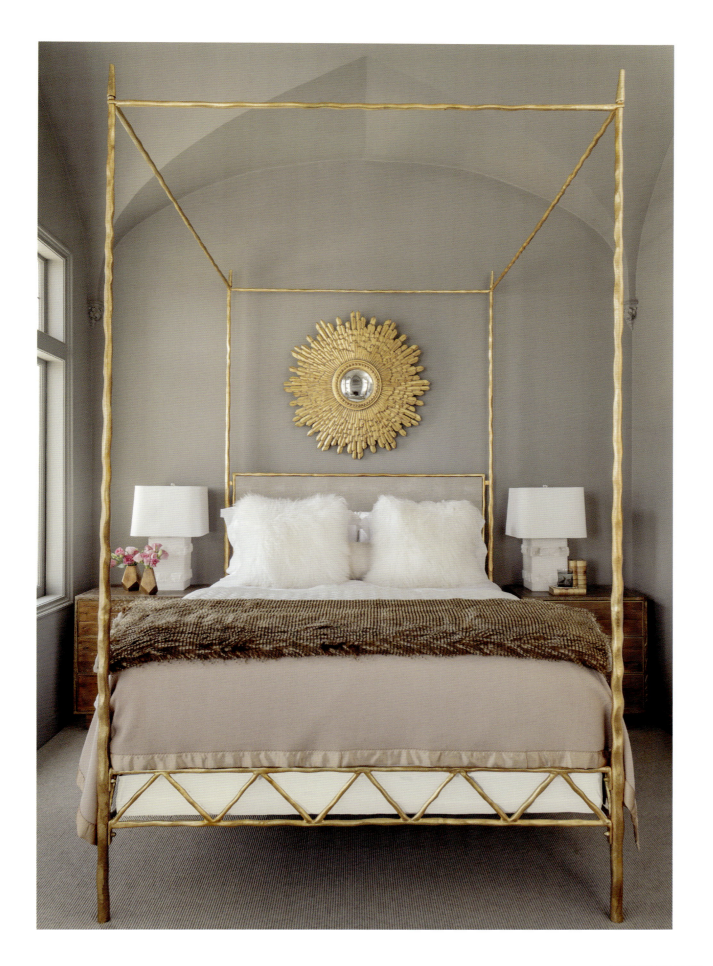

The home office is framed by French doors and an ornate wrought-iron balustrade.

GABRIELA GARGANO
A MAGICAL OASIS DEVELOPED OVER TIME

New York, USA

Nolita, or Little Italy as it's often referred to, is one of this writer's favorite neighborhoods. It has a strong community feel that one could also imagine in various Italian villages. Complete with bookshops, cafés, and specialty boutiques, this self-contained precinct seems to have it all. It certainly appealed to interior designer Gabriela Gargano and her husband, Rob, when they first inspected it. Rob (who was then her boyfriend) was searching for a two-bedroom apartment with outdoor space south of 23rd Street. "This apartment had an incredible homelike quality to it, feeling more like a house than an apartment," says Gabriela, whose apartment occupies the top two levels of the building, with an additional rooftop terrace and two generous balconies that lead from the kitchen and living areas. The generous natural light on both sides, one of which overlooks the historic former police building, also makes the home unique.

The couple purchased the apartment well before the neighborhood's gentrification, at a time when it was still fairly gritty. But given that Soho was just next door, they could see that it was only a matter of time before it would become a sought-after address. And although the bones of the apartment were good, the standard of finishes and fittings throughout was fairly ordinary. However, before making any changes, the couple lived in it for about six months while they established their design goals and, importantly, their budget.

While Gabriela didn't buy in a fine, heritage-listed building, she was still keen to understand its history—once a multilevel parking lot that had been transformed into five lofts in the early aughts. So, there were certainly no period moldings or decorative details to start with, but obviously it came with a certain minimalist and slightly industrial aesthetic. "There was a stillness to the space that I wanted to retain even though it's a fairly bustling part of the

@grisorostudio
grisorostudio.com
Photos by Kristen Francis

city (being on the higher levels offers a certain calmness)," says Gabriela, who enjoys looking over the low-rise buildings that surround her, predominantly four and five stories. "I wanted the interior to maintain that sense of stillness," she adds.

To achieve this quiet ambience, Gabriela selected a fairly neutral color palette of white, gray, black, wood, and steel accents that incorporated a lot of integrated storage so the home wouldn't feel cluttered. The fireplace in the living area was removed and the entire wall was finished in marble, framed by a bookcase, a wine fridge, and a bar. This move increased the home's functionality but did not detract from its open-plan feel. And rather than fill the home with only contemporary furniture, there's a combination of new and vintage pieces, along with art that's been collected over the years. "I prefer a room to develop over time without it feeling of a moment," says Gabriela, pointing out the Swedish chairs from the 1940s and the 1950s coffee table. The dining chairs are also Danish from the 1960s. She also opted

The main living area has a number of 1950s pieces, from armchairs to the multibranched central pendant light.

Opposite: French doors open to the terrace, complete with an al fresco dining setting.

Following spread: The dining room has built-in shelves adorned with paintings, photographs, and books.

for durable natural fabrics such as wool for the rugs and for the upholstery. And while there's a graphic color palette in the living areas, the main bedroom suite features warm taupe colors, with earthy brown upholstery and furnishings to create a more intimate feel.

Mindful of the origins of this loft-style apartment, Gabriela wanted to ensure a minimal and clean aesthetic throughout—with a slightly industrial style used for hardware. She even stripped the elevator doors to expose the original steel finish, to pay homage to the industrial origins of the building. However, this sharper edge is balanced with some softer silhouettes such as the lamps in the main bedroom by ceramicist Victoria Morris, with their unexpected proportions and speckled finish. Other finds include the mid-century chair that was found at one of her favorite vintage shops in the Hamptons. The photograph above the bed by Frank Schott also infuses the bedroom with greenery, perfect given that there wasn't much room for a potted plant.

Some of the best New York views can be enjoyed from the terrace.

While Gabriela and Rob inherited a fairly blank canvas, their main challenge was working with the apartment's unusual shape, including a number of angled walls that reflect the trapezoidal shape of the building. So, it was necessary to build things into some of the walls, which was costly but avoided creating lopsided rooms. Additional storage areas were also in short supply. And while the views and location are now highly coveted, the original fit-out was relatively spec-driven rather than thoughtfully stitched together—hence the former kitchen cabinetry was completely removed, as were the tiles in areas such as the bathroom, with a wall added in the bathroom to create a new closet.

Given the aspect from the living area and terrace, it's not surprising that it's here where the couple gravitates. As soon as the elevator doors open, they are in a light-filled living room framed by a verdant terrace. "It's a magical oasis in the city," says Gabriela, who worked closely with landscape designer Katonah Roots to create the terrace garden.

The kitchen is simple and contemporary, with soft grays and natural finishes.

TIPS

When it comes to selecting a paint color, using swatches can be tricky. I suggest painting sample boards and then looking at these in the actual room at various times of the day. White is of course the most challenging but, I would add, also the most important.

We find that often people try to include too many functions in each room, especially when they live in apartments. Space is of course at a premium for city dwellers, but too many times the guest room / playroom just ends up as a storage area and is not used to its full potential.

When it comes to storage, design it so that it's used efficiently, encouraging closet clean-outs and incorporating organizers when they're needed.

The scale of artwork is also important. Sometimes, even a small piece can add charm in a home.

The bathroom is layered with pictures. Even the floor is used to display art.

Opposite:
Top: A guest bedroom features simple finishes such as Roman-style blinds to increase the sense of space.

Bottom left: A few simple vases say enough.

Bottom right: A 1950s armchair is a perfect spot for reading.

Opposite: The soft tones continue into the main bedroom, accented by a 1950s bureau and chair.

Following spread: A nursery includes a 1950s armchair and lamp.

WESLEY MOON
ADDING A SENSE OF WARMTH

New York, USA

Wesley Moon's apartment in New York's Upper East Side is like a jewel box, richly furnished and sumptuously appointed. It perfectly suits the way he lives and how he likes to entertain. The location is also perfect for someone who is so familiar with the city, having lived here for twenty years. Previously, he lived in downtown Manhattan. "As much as I loved that time, I was ready for a more residential grown-up feeling," says Wesley, who settled on the Carnegie Hill area of the Upper East Side because it was quiet, convenient, and just a few blocks from Central Park and Museum Mile.

While the location is idyllic, the apartment itself was a little fragmented and, as Wesley says, "not user friendly." However, he could see how it could easily be reconfigured into his dream layout—including his needs for an open-plan living and dining room that would connect to a library. Wesley was also keen to draw upon the building's rich jazz moderne origins, built in 1939 just prior to the outbreak of World War II. "I wanted to make the apartment feel like it could have always been that way, at least architecturally, from day one," says Wesley, who also took inspiration from the artist Gustav Klimt, whose famous portrait of Adele Bloch-Bauer hangs in the Neue Galerie just a few blocks away. Other influences came from his love of history and his travels. In the dining area for example, he partnered with de Gournay to customize the wallpaper. Painted on gold leaf with matte pigments, the scene depicts the Maria Santissima del Carmelo in Palermo, with various flora and fauna from Sicily.

Although Wesley spends considerable time in the evening in his library, surrounded by his extensive book collection, and it being the only place with a television, he wanted all the rooms to be used—the library is also used as a guest room when needed. However, the main bedroom was enlarged and

Gold features prominently in this luxurious New York apartment, from the walls to the ornate lights and pelmets.

@wesleymooninc
www.wesleymoon.com
Photos by Pernille Loof

reworked to include a substantial walk-in dressing area and en suite—the entire suite can be completely sectioned off by closing concealed onyx doors.

Even though there are common threads in each room, one of the repeating ideas is the continuous color story, which provides a sense of cohesion throughout the apartment. "I still wanted to give each room its own flavor," says Wesley, who points out all the repeating colors in what appears to be the one hue. Some of Wesley's most treasured pieces can be found in the gallery and in the living room. An ornate tulipierre by Matthew Solomon from Maison Gerard creates a sense of arrival for guests as they enter his home. The centerpiece of the living room is an art deco–inspired marble fireplace, and above the mantel is a deconstructed portrait of Elizabeth by Michael Mapes, composed from hundreds of miniature photographs. Hidden in the work is a picture of Wesley's grandmother, also named Elizabeth. A Maria Berrio is also proudly displayed in the kitchen.

Sumptuous lounges and chairs bring a sense of luxe to the living room.

The apartment is richly endowed with objects d'art and paintings and is luxuriously appointed. However, when Wesley first inspected it, it had been stripped of all architectural detail and was simply a plain white box. "I wanted to restore the apartment's heritage but also make it contemporary at the same time," says Wesley, who incorporated many architectural details such as cover moldings and door castings that had been removed in the 1970s. One of the key drivers in this renovation was to add a sense of warmth, a place where friends and family would enjoy gathering. To add this warmth in the primary bedroom, for example, Wesley upholstered the walls in Toyine Sellers and Fortuny and commissioned Jane Henry, a decorative painter, to add squiggles of gold paint to the eighteenth-century tapestry that's displayed on the wall above the bed. "I never want a space to feel too precious. It should always feel lived in," he says.

One of the biggest challenges for Wesley was working with the solidity of the walls in the apartment, and making these changes during COVID-19 when getting things done would test most people working in the design industry—with delays at almost every step of the project. "You just need to roll with the punches."

The main living area has a marble fireplace and wide ceiling cornices.

TIPS

I think that people are often too safe when renovating their own home. They think solely about the resale value and don't think enough about themselves, when they are the ones living in the home.

People also tend to think that large rooms require large pieces of furniture. You can actually give the effect of the space feeling larger by using smaller-scale pieces and creating multiple seating areas.

People don't understand the importance of warm light. When selecting lighting (even if you are using LED), be sure that you are using color temperatures that will mimic incandescent lighting. Learn about warm dim in recessed fixtures, so that you can make a space feel more intimate during the evening.

The dining area is treated like a treasure trove.

The kitchen has extensive marble countertops and backsplashes, as well as a marble-tiled floor.

Curved windows accentuate the form of the building.

Opposite: A portrait of Dolly Parton, as featured in the library, who is one of the owner's heroes.

Opposite: The main bedroom is lavishly appointed.

Top left: Unexpected passages can be found in this apartment.

Above: A Fornasetti cabinet takes a place of pride in the home.

WESLEY MOON

Top left: Many of the original 1930s features have been retained.

Top right: Marble features extensively, with mirrors adding depth to the spaces.

Left: A walk-in wardrobe that takes the art of dressing to a new level—with extensive built-in joinery to accommodate everything from shoes to suits.

Opposite: Gilt furniture combined with Renaissance art adds to the apartment's charm.

DESIGNER DIRECTORY

Candace Barnes Design
www.candacebarnes.com
United States of America

B.E Architecture
www.bearchitecture.com
@b.e_architecture
Australia

Kate Challis Interiors
https://katechallis.com
@katechallisinteriors
Australia

Melissa de Campo
designconsigned.com.au
@designconsigned.com.au
Australia

Michael Del Piero
Michael Del Piero Good Design
michaeldelpiero.com
@michael_del_piero
United States of America

Tina Engelen
www.tinaengelen.com
Australia

Gabriela Gargano
grisorostudio.com
@grisorostudio
United States of America

Thomas Geerlings
Framework Studio
www.framework.eu
@frmwrkstudio
The Netherlands

Emily Gillis
www.emilygillis.com.au
@emilygillis
Australia

Sally Mackereth
Studio Mackereth
www.studiomackereth.com
@studiomackereth
United Kingdom

John Marx & Nikki Beach
Form4 Architecture
https://form4inc.com
@form4_architecture
United States of America

Dorothy Measer
dk designhouse
dkdesignhouse.com
United States of America

Wesley Moon, Inc.
www.wesleymoon.com
@wesleymooninc
United States of America

Andrew Parr
https://sjb.com.au
@_andrewparr
Australia

Allison Pye
www.pyeinteriors.com
@allisonpyeinteriors
Australia

Andrew Sheinman
Pembrooke & Ives
www.pembrookeandives.com
@pembrookeandives
United States of America

Tatjana Sprick
@tatjanasprick
Germany

Tim Van Steenbergen
timvansteenbergen.com
@timvansteenbergen
Belgium

Carole Whiting
www.carolewhiting.com
@carolewhiting
Australia

Vicente Wolf
vicentewolf.com
@vicentewolfdesigns
United States of America

ABOUT THE AUTHOR

Stephen Crafti has been writing about architecture and design for 30 years and has produced more than 45 books. He also writes for leading newspapers and magazines in Australia and overseas. In addition, Stephen leads architecture and design tours both in Australia and overseas with the leading cultural tour company Australians Studying Abroad (ASA). He also leads his own tours in Melbourne, where he resides with his partner in a home designed by architect Robert Simeoni. While they are not designers, with the assistance of furniture and lighting designer Suzie Stanford, they created a home that feels right for them.

Stephen Crafti and his cat Harvey in his own home renovated by architect Robert Simeoni. *Image courtesy of photographer Armelle Habib and the* Sunday Life *magazine,* The Age / Sydney Morning Herald